SELLING KEEPS YOU BROKE.

SELLING KEEPS YOU BROKE.

A **HOLISTIC** APPROACH TO **DISRUPTIVE SALES PERFORMANCE** TO EARN **BIG**.

Selling Keeps You Broke.
A **Holistic** Approach to **Disruptive Sales Performance** to Earn **Big**.

E-Book ISBN: 979-8-9880981-1-9
Paperback ISBN: 979-8-9880981-0-2
Cover Design by: Kash Hasworth
Illustrations by: Kash Hasworth

DEDICATION

This book is dedicated to my superhero wife, Laura, our exceptional trio of children–Skylin, Harlan, and Krew–as well as the countless friends, mentors, and hundreds of sales warriors and leaders I've had the honor of crossing swords with in the battlefield of business. Each chapter has been meticulously crafted with my children in mind, arming them with the knowledge and strategies they'll need to conquer the complexities of life and secure financial victories even when I'm no longer by their side to guide them.

You four are the driving force that ignites my unwavering pursuit of financial freedom, while the multitude of talented individuals I've encountered have enriched my arsenal with invaluable insights and expertise that have shaped the wisdom shared within these pages. To all the sales gladiators and leaders who have enhanced my journey, thank you for your collective knowledge and for helping me turn this book into a battle-tested guide.

My deepest gratitude goes out to each and every one of you, and I hope this book serves as a testament to the power of collaboration, tenacity, and relentless discipline that enables the sales community to ascend to levels of disruption to create an everlasting impact. Here's to the enduring legacy we will forge together.

Learn. Elevate. Disrupt.

CONTENTS

INTRODUCTION

Okay, of course, the idea of selling by itself doesn't make you broke.

In fact, one can argue that selling isn't everything, it's the only thing. After all, everything we do revolves around selling in some form or fashion. However, having an obsession with selling could be more damaging than helpful. You see, selling is simple – it's bringing clear, consistent, and honest communication to the table to persuade someone to buy a product, service, or idea.

The challenge is, salespeople who obsess over selling tend to overcomplicate the simplicity in the art of selling and prioritize it over other more important elements that disruptive performance requires.

Now, if you're anything like me, you're thinking, *"well, of course, selling isn't the most important thing, **closing** is."*

You're exactly right.

That'd be hard to deny due to the widespread belief that closing is the only thing that matters in sales ever since Alec Baldwin introduced his ABC (Always Be Closing) sales strategy in the 1992 film "Glengarry Glen Ross". He quotes *"Only one thing counts in this life. Get them to sign on the line which is dotted."*[1]

However, the most successful salespeople know that closing is only **one** component when it comes to high-level performance. If you want to really stand amongst the best in their respective field, you have to not only master the close, but two other critical components that are equally important.

In this book, I unpack a host of best practices, guiding principles, and a multi-dimensional approach to success that is designed to completely disrupt the laws of the average.

What could you do with the comprehensive winning formula for elite sales results?

For me, that question came with an easy answer. It was purely to buy more time to do what I wanted when I wanted. Freedom is my definition of the ultimate level of success – the freedom to do what you love. As I obsessed over my journey to a comfortable level of freedom, I became consumed by optimizing every part of my life to make it possible so that I could enjoy it without having to worry if taking time away from the grind would jeopardize my standard of living.

Broken down in a series of parts, I share the Triple C Path to Victory that I've used to earn that freedom – as well as training hundreds of salespeople and business owners throughout my career, many of whom had little to no sales experience and developed into some of the most results-oriented leaders and salespeople in their respective industry.

As we dive in, like with any information, the material is only as valuable as the length at which it's practiced and applied. With that being said, are you ready to take your results to the next level?

PART 1

PART 1:

PREPARATION FOR GREATNESS

CHAPTER 1

MINDSET MATTERS

At the heart of top performance is the mind that conquers the result. Elite performers across every profession, department, or industry, from professional sports players to sales reps, have mastered their most important asset – their minds. This includes how they think, how they train themselves to react to a challenge or obstacle, their daily habits and disciplines, and all that comes with mental fortitude.

Take it from one of the most physically demanding sports professionals, Steph Curry, who said, *"If I can train my mind to be there and to be sharp, it's just as important as being there physically.*" He said, "*when that's in sync, when I'm confident, the sky's the limit*"[1]. There's a reason why the phrase "*Get your head in the game*" is so overused. Because the fact is, if you master your mind, you master your reality. So it seems, our reality is only a reflection of our thoughts that live with us daily.

Starting out my career in the wireless industry, I had an innate understanding of this idea. I would visualize where I desired to be. As a result, everything I consumed would revolve around breathing life into that vision.

As I started out as an entry-level sales rep in this shabby little kiosk inside of a dying mall, I knew that wouldn't last for long. I was destined for an executive-level position that would allow me to gain exposure and build the skills necessary to be a business owner one day myself. I didn't care about my age, experience, education, or even existing layers of leadership that were in place. I had the grit to learn whatever I needed and the work ethic to outperform my peers in an effort to excel rapidly.

Because of this internal eagerness to learn and grow, it would show itself in the form of self-education and initiative. I understood that if I was going to advance, I better master each role on the way up. So, I set out to be the best damn salesperson that the company had seen.

Within a couple of weeks, I was finally getting a feel for the products, the service, and the efforts that had to go into generating leads. I would spend the 11-hour days testing different approaches to bypassing traffic, printing flyers for surrounding businesses to share and practicing the point-of-sale process for when the opportunity finally came.

On my second Sunday on the job, it was incredibly slow. I was already getting frustrated with the results I had seen thus far. Even though I had trained with one of the most talented salespeople in the company, I started to question my delivery. *"I literally wrote down and memorized his entire pitch, verbatim. I'm working with the same traffic he has success with. What in the hell is the problem here?"*, I said to myself.

Doing everything but banging my head against the wall, I was ready for the day to be over with. With just an hour or so left before closing, this gentleman returned that I had spoken to a week prior. As he approached the kiosk, I started to get butterflies. I quickly realized that's a giddy roiling in the pit of your stomach when a sale is about to take place. Trying to contain myself, he approached the counter, set the brochure down in front of me that I had written down his quote on and said, "can you port over from Verizon?".

"Absolutely!" I exclaimed. *"Do you have your account number?"*, I said. Then, his credit failed.

Kidding. That would have shattered my soul and I probably wouldn't be here today to tell the story. He left with five new phones and a successful port over from his old carrier! It was from that transaction that I knew those butterflies were evidence that I was truly in love with the process of selling.

As I went into the next week, the seeds were sprouting and flowers were blooming. I started doing several accounts a week and ended the year as the top salesperson in the company with only eight months of selling.

Years later, the owner, which is now considered close family and still a mentor of mine, revealed that that very Sunday was scheduled to be my last day. He thought I wasn't cut out for sales. Boy, was he wrong.

KEY TAKEAWAY

Throughout this experience, I was able to extract a powerful lesson – as long as you're making progress, trust the process. Success might not show up at the rate you desire, but the universe is designed to reward those that seed the land.

Within the year, I had taken on managing two of our local retail locations. The company was looking to expand to a city about three hours away. I volunteered to take on the opening since it wasn't a sought-after task for most. For me, I saw it as an opportunity to show my ability to recruit, train and sustain a healthy sales team that can operate in my absence. I packed my bags and headed for Charlottesville, VA.

This was my true test to myself to see how I could perform in a city that was foreign to me. At the time, we didn't have any local staffing support to relieve me or the staff, once in place. So, as I interviewed, I knew I wasn't there to find a team of sales reps. I was there to replace my leadership that could construct a team of sales reps. Someone that had the drive, ambition, and leadership personality to take ownership of the location to manage it successfully. Or else, I'd be subject to being the store manager myself when my role was to have more of a regional presence.

After countless interviews, I over-hired and invested in several reps. When they genuinely care about seeing your team win by giving them the guidance and the tools necessary to be successful, you get the best version of people. This helped me identify the leader in the pack and continued to pour my time and energy into their development. After a month or so, we had successfully fine-tuned the roster.

With one ground-up location under my belt, I was eager to tackle any challenge. After a series of top-performing locations, I quickly earned a VP of Sales spot in the company. With the leadership sales team we had established across our footprint, the owner and I went on to aggressively build 28 locations across four states, becoming the number one dealer by sales volume for the wireless carrier year after year.

These collective accomplishments were made possible by a strong team of leaders that possessed a fierce mindset to win. When you can tap into that mindset, and show others how to do it as well, you get your greatest results – from a performance perspective, from an operations perspective, and from an overall quality perspective.

Prior to the wireless industry, I didn't have a job. Selling phones was really my first real job at age 21. I didn't even complete high school. I was grounded in a much different environment for most of my adolescent years, and the corporate space was something that was really foreign to me. My mother and my father never had a corporate job. My mother was pregnant with me at age 14 and dropped out of high school shortly after. She's been a waitress most of her life. My father was a hustler. He's served 15 years or so in prison on and off since I was a kid. While both of them heavily supported me and helped shape who I am today, I share that to say that my network wasn't my way into the industry. A degree didn't assist or catapult me to the forefront of the industry. What I would say has been most impactful is the mindset that I've carried leading up to and throughout my career.

Unless you have the right mindset, there's no right amount of sales training or mentorship that's going to take you to the forefront of your space.

CHAPTER 2

Toss The Split Wires

The most successful people in the world focus intensely on their inner circle. Why? Because success is in your association. Surrounding yourself with accomplished people allows you to extract the insights that contributed to their achievements. Consequently, you begin to grow and inch closer to your goals as you progress through a number of milestones. Soon enough, you attain objectives that initially seemed distant, or weren't even included in your initial vision, all thanks to the guidance of the right mentors.

You see, we absorb information from the people we're exposed to and interact with through social learning. As humans, we are inherently social beings who learn from observing and imitating others. Our brains are wired to process and store information gathered from our surroundings, including the people we encounter. This is great when you're surrounded by positive influences and a fierce circle of winners.

But here's the thing, the same principle holds true in the reverse. The same social learning process that helps us acquire positive traits can also lead to the adoption of detrimental behaviors.

Have you ever had one of your phone charging cables develop split wires at the neck? If not, imagine grappling with a malfunctioning phone cable with frayed wires near the connector. All you want is to charge your phone, but these pesky broken wires keep disconnecting the charge and reconnecting the charge – disconnecting, reconnecting, disconnecting, reconnecting. You fiddle with it, hoping the problem just goes away. You've got somewhere to be. It's 8 AM and you have to be out the door by 10 AM, and your battery is at a measly 10%. The temptation to sling the charger across the room is strong.

But instead of abandoning it, you're compelled to stick with it. You bend it every which way. You twist and turn the charger, seeking that sweet little awkward position that restores the connection. When that fails, determined, you resort to using black tape to secure the connection, and the charging icon finally lights up. An hour passes. You go to swipe your phone before heading out the door, only to discover your phone's charge has dwindled instead of increased.

That's exactly how having the wrong people around you works. There may be sparks of charge here and there, but they're a net negative in your life. Their drama, their negativity, and their lack of effort rub off on you, depleting your energy reserves. And unless you replace your charger altogether, that negative charge is going to keep draining your battery until it reaches total depletion.

This is because our emotional state is susceptible to the influence of those around us, a phenomenon known as emotional contagion[1]. Just as we can absorb positivity, enthusiasm, and motivation from uplifting individuals, we can also experience drained energy when associating with negative people. Their pessimism, complaints, or lack of ambition can permeate our thoughts and emotions, leading to a decrease in our overall well-being and productivity.

To foster personal growth and maintain our emotional equilibrium, it's crucial to be mindful of the information we choose to be around as our ongoing circle of influence. By intentionally choosing positive influences and distancing ourselves from negative ones, we can optimize our potential and maximize the benefits of social learning. So, if you're sick of battling it out with those split wires, toss 'em. Your future self will thank you for your renewed energy, focus, self-confidence, and thirst for ambitious goals.

KEY TAKEAWAY

Total depletion is not a state anyone wants to be in that has places to go. You have to be charged up. Surround yourself with those that contribute to your charge and not deplete it.

The Direction of Energy Evaluation Checklist

The people in our lives are always charging us or draining us, sometimes without even being conscious of it. Knowing the traits that control the direction of our energy is important to our mental state and overall success.

This checklist will help you assess whether the people in your life are energizing your aspirations or draining your potential. Our social environment plays a crucial role in shaping our thoughts, habits, and overall well-being. Surrounding ourselves with individuals who empower and uplift us is essential for personal growth and success as we take on a disruptive approach to sales performance. Conversely, maintaining relationships with those who hinder our progress can be detrimental to our emotional and mental health.

This evaluation checklist will guide you through a series of criteria to determine if your circle of influence is contributing to your charge, acting as a positive force in your life, or depleting it, by holding you back and stifling your potential. By carefully examining the impact of each relationship, you'll gain valuable insights into the dynamics at play and be equipped to make informed decisions about the connections you cultivate.

This person never seems to be going anywhere in life

This person never challenges themselves or you

This person always has something to complain about

This person has an excuse for everything and never takes ownership

This person never takes action, and expects things to come to him

This person will often take credit when they can, even if not earned

This person does not have a healthy routine and spends their days aimlessly

This person has a hard time finding information on their own, and expects it to be handed to them

This person is always the victim

This person has a general poor attitude

How many boxes did you check?

Is this person **DEPLETING** your charge?

This person has a growth mindset – they're always learning

This person has knowledge that can help me achieve my goals

This person has experienced a greater level of success in an area I care about

This person shares similar values with me

This person holds a very strong belief that you either find a way or make a way

This person will often encourage, motivate and challenge me

This person will hold me accountable

This person is someone I would hire, work for or partner with

This person is value oriented – they're always providing me with value

This person always has a positive perspective on life

How many boxes did you check?

Is this person **CONTRIBUTING** to your charge?

As you count up the positives and negatives in the evaluation of your inner circle, it will help you identify if the people you associate with are contributing to your success or holding you back. This assessment is not meant to dictate severing ties with certain individuals but rather to offer valuable insights into who deserves your time and attention if you aspire to lead a life filled with positivity, health, and abundance.

2 OF MY MOST VALUED TRAITS OF ALL

Out of all the traits of positively charging people, there are two most distinctive ones I've witnessed top performers possess that experience extraordinary success.

POSITIVE PERSPECTIVE

The first is a positive perspective. Perspective is an incredibly powerful tool that is the cornerstone of one's success. When you come across people that have a refreshingly satisfying perspective, especially in the midst of difficult situations, you're likely in the company of someone that can contribute greatly to your charge.

Take your dream beach destination, for example. Skilled photographers can shoot every angle of that destination in a light that captures the essence of its beauty that immediately evokes feelings of warmth, happiness, and a strong desire to book that flight immediately. Conversely, if someone hates the beach, their photos would likely deliver an image that doesn't spark any exciting emotion at all due to its dullness and lack of creativity to capture the essence of everything that speaks to you.

Similarly, just as each photographer's work can shape your perspective in a single image – your upbringing, experiences and mental and physical health has shaped your perspective. All of these contributing factors to perspective also mean it can be influenced and transformed entirely. So, even if you don't have the most positive perspective yourself, it can be changed.

TENACIOUS RESOLVE

The second, and arguably the most powerful trait, is a relentless pursuit to make things happen. If you struggle with maintaining a positive perspective, that tends to be reshaped when you start accomplishing your goals by powering through the excuses. Again, experience shapes perspective.

In the workforce, there are two very distinct people: those that find an excuse and those that find a way. Many that have adopted this approach have eliminated the thought of another destination that's short of where they really want to go. There is no other destination but the destination that they have set out to arrive at. The strategy may change along the way, but where they're going remains the same.

In every aspect of your life, when you apply this uncompromising approach, you will outwork and outperform everyone around you. Why, because there's an excuse for everything and it's an easy way out. People take advantage of those excuses more times than not, and as a result, their performance suffers, their work suffers, and their relationships suffer.

If you've never heard of Captain Hernán Cortés, the Spanish conquistador known for sailing to Mexico to conquer the Aztecs, it's one that has resonated with me for years. After ignoring orders from his home country, he and his men set out to overthrow the ruler settled in the capital of Tenochtitlan. Upon arrival, with over 500 men and 11 ships, his first order was to burn the ships[2]. I'm sure you're thinking what I thought which was "... *and then his men killed him immediately*". But apparently, his team was just as crazy as he was and they actually burned the ships.

It was clear that he was only willing to accept victory. It was either that, or die. Because of this starkly drawn line in the sand, it stirred up immense amounts of resourcefulness and relentlessness that otherwise would have not been brought to the surface in his men. This ultimately led to a victorious takeover.

When you adopt this "There is no option B" rule into your life, you make a commitment to yourself that you'll figure out how to achieve the task at hand no matter how complex or daunting it may seem. The result will be that you'll continue to rise above those that chose to make an excuse.

In conclusion, embracing these two powerful traits and incorporating them into your life will pave the way for remarkable achievements and personal growth.

As you adopt a positive perspective, you'll begin to view challenges as opportunities for growth, rather than setbacks. This shift in mindset will enable you to approach difficulties with resilience and resourcefulness. Moreover, surrounding yourself with individuals who share this optimistic outlook will reinforce your commitment to cultivating a positive attitude.

In summary, assessing your inner circle and surrounding yourself with positive, driven individuals will provide the foundation for personal and professional growth. By embracing the traits of a positive perspective and relentless pursuit, you'll equip yourself with the tools needed to thrive in the face of adversity and rise above any limitations.

Remember, the journey toward success begins with your mindset and the company you keep. Choose your circle wisely, nurture these powerful traits, and watch as your life transforms into one filled with positivity, achievement, and abundance.

CHAPTER 3

Subconscious Transformation

In order to really master the elite mindset, you have to really go through a subconscious transformation. You have to recreate your habits and truly believe that you're going to get where you want to be with every 100 trillion+ cells that make up your body. When I started out in sales, I was part-time, I was a sales rep, brand new to the industry, and I told myself that I was going to lead that organization one day. At the time, we had so many layers of leadership in place already that, to the average individual, it could have been discouraging to set such an ambitious goal.

Then, I achieved it.

And then, the goals got bigger. I set out to create an online platform that facilitated relationships with incarcerated men and women to the outside world in an effort to expose them to new information that can change their outlook and reality. Knowing absolutely nothing about coding or website design, I became obsessive over absorbing information to help me achieve it. That led to a partnership with a longtime friend that shared my passion. InTouch for Inmates was born. What was once a single thought, led to thousands of connections and national television attention by joining a panel on The Doctor's TV Show to discuss our mission.

That success led to other business ventures and the size of the goals just started to grow with each milestone on the road to financial freedom.

Being a kid from the streets that never completed high school, and whose only formal education was a prison-issued GED from Buckingham Correctional Center at the age of 17, these results don't seem typical. But my perspective was I wasn't going to allow the limitations of the outside world to be the voice of my inside world.

I had convinced myself that it was possible through a constant conditioning of believing and executing.

We've been programmed to accept average. "Be realistic". That's what most of us have heard our entire life, right?

So when we have these grand ideas and thoughts enter into our brain that contradict our programming, our subconscious mind – that's the part of the mind that you're unaware of and where the programming is stored – it kicks it back and sends an emotional message throughout our body that brings fear, uncertainty, disbelief, and anxiety.

The most exciting thing is we can reprogram, or recondition our minds to think at a greater level, but you have to trust the process, you have to stay disciplined, and you have to stay the course. This doesn't just apply to sales, it's something you can apply throughout your life to generate greater results and live on your own terms.

Check this out - here's a diagram conceptualized by a guy named Dr. Thurman Fleet[1]. This will help you understand exactly how your mind and body work to create the results that are our reality.

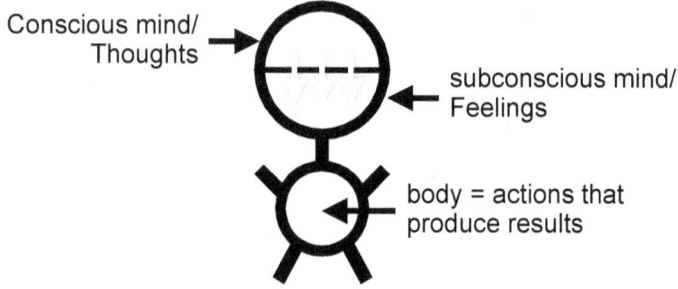

We have two parts to our mind: the conscious mind and the subconscious.

Our conscious mind is where our thoughts take place. It's where we make decisions. It's our current awareness.

Our subconscious mind is where our beliefs, memories, and feelings are stored. This is where our programming is stored - how we were conditioned throughout our life.

Our conscious mind naturally likes thoughts that are in harmony with our subconscious mind. Why, because those thoughts give us a sense of comfort. It's what we're used to. So it makes sense that when you have a foreign idea enter your conscious mind, your subconscious pushes it away and moves you back into your comfort zone – that place of safety.[2]

So the question becomes - how do you reprogram your subconscious to reach that elite mindset?

SUBCONSCIOUS REPROGRAMMING

If your reality is a reflection of your thoughts, how do the two come together? When you create a thought, your thoughts are what create your conditionings and your habits. This is because your thoughts create feelings. These thoughts communicate with your body and your body takes action to get the results that you created in your mind. And this is what shapes our reality.

Have you ever created a scenario in your head that immediately made you angry? It reminds me of those "what your woman thinks you're doing with the boys versus what you're really doing with the boys" videos. The woman imagines a night filled with strippers, drinking, and belligerent behavior. And then the view flips to what the boys are actually doing when she uninvitingly arrives – two playing NFL on the PlayStation while the other two are playing hot hands and forcing the losers to eat the cold pepperoni pizza and wings that's been sitting on the counter for the last four days. That's a small-scale example, but the woman created an entire negative scenario in her head that evoked emotion that led her to take action.

So if you want to change your reality, you have to change your conditioning and your habits, and this is done with your thoughts. This is where the reprogramming starts.

STEP ONE

The beginning of your reprogramming is to get so zoomed in on that desired outcome that you can see it on a molecular level.

Now, notice I said the outcome and not the goal. Your goal might be to become the most successful salesperson in your space, your industry, or period, right? But what's the desired outcome? What are you looking to get out of achieving that goal? Maybe you want more financial freedom so you can travel when you like. Maybe it's that you want to have the experience to train others so you can transform other people's lives. Maybe it's just that you like to dominate and you want to be known as the authority in your industry. No matter your personal reasons, you have to clearly define what that desired outcome looks like for you.

STEP TWO

Once you have a clear picture of your desired outcome, you identify and tackle the obstacles - the fears, the self-image, and the behavioral patterns that have held you back. It has to be merciless collusion.

As an example: maybe it's this patterned thought that every time becoming an authority in your industry pops into your mind, fear sets in and you go back to that comfort zone and abort the mission. *That* is what you have to tackle. So you would identify that as an obstacle.

You identify that obstacle, that pattern, that behavior, and then you attack it like a lioness that just witnessed a group of hyenas attempting to harm your cub.

You may need some time with your thoughts to identify what that obstacle or behavior is that's existing as the divider wall between you and greatness. I've created a guide that'll map out an action plan for the reprogramming of your subconscious. If you can identify those items, commit to following the replacement patterns and it'll help you overcome many behaviors that you may not even be aware of.

STEP THREE

You have to get your message into this subconscious mind tunnel. In order to change a habit or conditioning, there has to be constant exposure. To get into the subconscious, there has to be repetition.

Minimal exposure leads to short-term memory. And on average, our short-term memory only stores around seven pieces of information for 20 or 30 seconds. That's why most people forget the name of the person they just met.

Long-term memory, as you obviously know, can store information for years or an entire lifetime. Now, some long-term memories are because of the emotion attached to that experience. But repetition, that continual exposure, can achieve the same result.[3]

In the beginning, change is going to be difficult. You've been walking this same pathway for years. When you create a new route, an untraveled pathway, there's going to be twigs, fallen trees and branches, and spider webs. The path is going to be narrow and uncomfortable. Get over it. Push through it. Make your way. The more frequently you visit that pathway, the more clear that pathway is going to be. The more familiar you're going to be with that pathway. And over time, you're going to be able to walk that trail with your eyes closed.

That's identical to how long-term memories are formed. The more frequently that memory travels that neural pathway, the more it's strengthened and permanent.[4]

On the following pages, I've included a workbook to kickstart your subconscious reprogramming. It's a 3 step approach to a subconscious transformation. Execute the practices daily. It includes meditation and a set of daily routines, and it works. Bridgewater Associates founder, Ray Dalio, the largest hedge fund in the world, said "Meditation has probably been the single most important reason for whatever success I've had."[5] The LinkedIn founder, Oprah, Russell Simmons, Tim Ferris, and a ton of entrepreneurs, multi-millionaires, and billionaires have these daily routines that helped them achieve greater levels of success.

If you want to think and perform like the elite, you have to replicate the practices that the elites use. Start it today with zero procrastination. You are the elite. Act like it.

STEP 1

My Goal

Desired Outcome #1

Desired Outcome #2

Desired Outcome #3

Desired Outcome #4

Desired Outcome #5

STEP 2

IDENTIFYING THE FEARS, SELF IMAGE AND BEHAVIOR PATTERNS THAT
YOUR SUBCONSCIOUS MIND IS STORING THAT IS HOLDING YOU BACK

The Behavior

The Trigger

The Fear Of

The Replacement Habit

EXAMPLE

THE BEHAVIOR
I tell myself I can't speak confidently
when faced with public speaking

THE BEHAVIOR TRIGGER
Emotional state when someone
asks me to speak

THE FEAR
Rejection/humiliation

THE REPLACEMENT HABIT
Be the first to volunteer to speak

STEP 3

TRANSFORMATION SCHEDULE

IDENTIFYING THE FEARS, SELF IMAGE AND BEHAVIOR PATTERNS THAT YOUR SUBCONSCIOUS MIND IS STORING THAT IS HOLDING YOU BACK

NIGHTLY ROUTINE — BEFORE SLEEP

15 MINUTES OF DESIRED OUTCOME QUESTIONS, THOUGHTS AND REQUESTS

Spend all of this time thinking about and discussing your goals and desired outcomes.

"Never go to sleep without a request to your subconscious." — Thomas Edison

MORNING ROUTINE — 10 MINUTES OF WALKING

10 MINUTES OF CLARITY MEDITATION
- Go to a quiet place within the first 10 minutes of waking up
- Meditate for mental clarity
  - Close your eyes
  - Focus on your breathing

10 MINUTES OF JEWEL JOTTING

- Document all new precious thoughts related to your goals and desired outcome on your 'Morning Routine Sheet'

"The morning is when your conscious mind is in its most active and creative state."

PERIODIC ROUTINE — 3X REPEATED AFFIRMATIONS

REPEAT AFFIRMATIONS AT LEAST 3 TIMES A DAY & THEN GO DO!

- Support your affirmations by taking the actions you're speaking into existence.

"Always replace "I can" and "I will" with "I am" to create the new belief you desire"

AFFIRMATIONS

Affirmations are reinforced thoughts that strike courage to take action. Without the action, the affirmation itself is just a lie you tell yourself every day to feel like you're being productive. While there's power in affirmations, the true subconscious transformation takes place from the habitual actions you begin to take from those affirmations. These courageous actions instill familiarity and confidence to convert discomfort into comfort. And as you continue to challenge deeper levels of the unknown and discomfort, the more you push beyond the comfort zone the average performers live in.

I am the creator of my own opportunities. I conquer all challenges. I build. I grow. I win. I prosper. I give to all walks of life. I inspire the uninspired. I challenge the unchallenged. I breathe abundance into the life of others and reach with limitless reach. I fight. I'm focused. I'm authentic. I'm caring. I live for greatness and lead for the difference. I am me.

Nice work getting through Part I. Now that you have a roadmap to mastering your mind, it's time to step into the Triple C Path to Victory.

PART 2:

THE CREATOR

THE CREATORS RULE

As I was building out sales teams early in my career, I became growingly frustrated with the lack of comprehensive resources in three core verticals. Because when people usually think of selling, their mind goes to the sales process. It goes to closing. It goes to customer service. While those areas are critically important, you will never reach your greatest potential unless you have incorporated The Creator role into who you are as a salesperson and you blend it with the other two, which are the Closer and the Care Champ.

So let's get right into it.

First of all, what is The Creator? Simply put, A creator creates and maximizes opportunities. Period. Now, what you'll extract from this Part is a closer look into the role of the Creator – how you can master creating and maximizing opportunities, sales opportunities specifically.

CREATOR MAKEUP

Let's start with the makeup of The Creator. This role consists of two parts:

THE CREATOR IS THE GO-GETTER.

They have optimized their mind to look for and go after an opportunity in every single situation. They have this go-get-it mentality. If traffic is nonexistent, it's the creator that finds ways to drive traffic into the store to generate leads and interest.

THE CREATOR IS CREATIVE.

They understand the importance of marketing, so they're always looking to enhance their marketing skills. This is an important component because we all know that many industries are ever-changing. In the solar industry, for example, you have tons of solar panel manufacturers each competing to make them more efficient with more attractive warranties, backup technology advancing, financing terms and fees constantly being adjusted, customer promotions being swapped out, etc.

As the creator, you have to take those products to market. If you have zero marketing skills, and you lack the ability to find people to get their attention, what happens? You get poor results.

THE CREATOR'S RULE

As the go-getter, The Creator's primary role is to find, create and maximize leads that are then converted to customers.

The idea of this role seems fairly simple, yet only a few tend to perform at disruptive levels. Wouldn't any employee or business owner naturally have this approach? Well, not exactly. And the reason is just as simple.

The number one reason why people don't master this role is purely from this reason alone – inaction.

You see, the most talented and successful leaders in the world can give you their step-by-step roadmap, best practices, and even contacts to help connect the dots.

But even with a precisely drawn blueprint, it would be of no value if no action is taken.

This brings me to the number one rule: **the creator must take massive action**. No matter how uncomfortable, no matter how easy it is to make an excuse, you have to make a commitment to yourself. Your spouse, closest friends, mentors, and motivators can't want it for you more than you want it for yourself. The laws of the universe aren't designed that way.

Action is the only route to experience, confidence, and explosive results.

Inaction is the literal opposite.

Inaction is paralysis.

The easiest way to action is to first understand what typically causes inaction. If you're failing to take action, you can attribute it to one or more of the following:

YOU DON'T CARE ENOUGH

If you find yourself not caring enough, it's likely because you're not passionate about the subject.

Those that truly want to join the top 1% have to be infatuated with the idea and commit to taking action. The fact that you're reading this should tell you that you do care enough.

YOU'RE FEARFUL

You have fear of change, failure, judgment, inadequacy, rejection, and/or uncertainty.

There are 7 billion people in the world, and I assure you that every single one of them experiences fear. It's a natural response to protect you from danger. But, when you go to call a lead, negotiate with a potential vendor, pitch an investor, or present to an audience, and you start to experience fear of rejection or uncertainty in your delivery, it's not going to jeopardize your life. It's not going to jeopardize your livelihood. You are not going to die. You have to change your perspective. Maybe that customer doesn't buy and that investor turns you down. But every experience serves a purpose. With every customer interaction, your conversation gets better. Your objection handling improves. Your fear diminishes.

I'm faced with fear constantly. I'm not the brightest guy in the room, so a fear I experience on occasion is a fear of uncertainty, especially when I take on an overwhelming project that requires specialized knowledge.

I've found that the only manageable approach to this fear is to buckle down and get started somewhere. That's when I pull out a physical notepad or my MacBook to start documenting whatever comes to mind. Here's an inside look into my process:

1. I will usually start with identifying what I specifically need to accomplish, breaking it down into bitesize pieces that seem more manageable to attack.

2. One by one, I'll absorb as much information as I can about each bitesize piece from multiple online resources – YouTube videos, articles, and

any reliable source of information I stumble across.

3. Once I feel like I have a general understanding, I'll find an expert that has the experience to confirm or expand on the research that I've found on my own.

   Pro tip: It's important to do your research before you reach out to an expert for direction. I learned this the hard way while getting embarrassed in the process. I went to one of my mentors for something that felt over my head. His reply was, *"Did you Google it?"*. Then it hit me, my hand on my forehead, that is. *"Of course, I didn't. I wanted the lazy way out and to waste your time in the process"*, I said to myself. Mentors and experts are more willing to help when they can tell you've put forth some time into trying to find answers on your own.

4. After I've gathered a general idea, I develop how I'm going to achieve whatever is it I planned to achieve. This leads me to personally do the work,

or outsource the work if the time it'll take me to learn the specialized knowledge doesn't align with my timeline.

For example, if you're in need of a complex website that will require coding, you'll be able to get more done faster by having a general understanding of the project and the skills needed to accomplish it so that you can interview a qualified developer to code it for you.

5. Finally, I get started on the actual work – doing it myself or interviewing freelancers to complete the work for me.

YOU'RE WAITING FOR THE RIGHT TIME

If you're waiting on the right time or opportunity, I have some good news and bad news for you. The bad news is there is never a right time or opportunity. There is only action and inaction. There is success and there is regret. There is now and there is never. The good news is you don't have to wait to start taking action.

As the decorated battlefield commander and admired leader George Patton once said, *"A good plan violently executed now is better than a perfect plan executed next week."*[1]

If you've ever asked Google a question, you've likely found an answer on Reddit through its community of 52 million, and counting, active users.[2]

However, they weren't always hailed as the "front page of the internet"[3] with billions of visits. In fact, in 2005, they had zero, their site looked like it was designed in Microsoft Word 2000, and its rules to protect its community were confusingly written.

The founders were faced with a decision – they could wait until the site was perfect for organic traffic to flow in, and have an interface users loved so they wouldn't have the need for its users to stick around for its evolution – or – create massive amounts of fake accounts to create a sense of community to jumpstart their vision. They chose to fake it until they made it. The Reddit founds took their overly simplistically designed platform and let their fake accounts aggressively grow the tone and direction they had envisioned until it was no longer needed.[4]

That single decision to act now instead of later, powering through this notion that you must wait for the right time, is what greatly contributed to them becoming the most-visited website on the internet.

Perfection is a progress killer. Unless you're a surgeon, it's better to cut twice and not measure than to measure twice and cut once.

CHAPTER 5

THE FOUR ELEMENTS OF COMMUNICATION

I cannot emphasize enough how important and impactful attention to your communication is in your sales process, from your first impression piece of marketing to maintaining your relationships with your customers long-term. There are four forms of communication that will allow you to gain buy-in and likeness from anything that will elevate your sales success. As a creator, this skill is at the very front of your process. It's your first impression. It's how you're perceived from the initial contact to years to come. And you need to be perceived as someone who is an expert, who is confident, who is trustworthy, and who is likable. No matter your role within your organization, you have to understand the power of these four elements. I want to share with you what they are and some best practices that will make your presentation better, make you more likable, and be able to close more sales. As the creator, you're setting yourself up for the close, but if you never get to the close, you never make any sales or connections to bring revenue into your company.

When we're communicating with the intent to get buy-in, we have to focus on, one, our spoken words, which are just the words that we are actually saying, two, the articulation of those words, which is the clarity and pronunciation of the words, three, the tonality, which is the pitch of your voice, the speed, and the rhythm, and four, the body language, which is hand gestures, eye contact, posture, and facial expressions.

Here's an example of how communication can have an effect on your experience as a consumer. Imagine, you enter a retail store to buy a new phone. The sales guy doesn't have a single customer in the store, he's slouched over in his seat, and he greets you sitting down. What's your perception of this guy already? The guy is slouched over, he didn't care about you enough to stand up, and you likely have already decided, based on the cues, that you have very little confidence in this guy to help you or be likable. But, before you leave, you decide that you're going to at least take a brochure to get some information to read over later. As you reach for the brochure, you see a promotional poster that triggers your interest, so you proceed to ask him about it. When the guy goes to answer, he sounds like Ben Stein from the Clear Eyes commercial. His delivery sounds like he has the personality of a piece of cardboard.

If you're anything like me, you have an appreciation for solid salesmanship, and you'd rather take your business elsewhere. Let's face it, If he doesn't put forth any effort in before you buy from him, you can safely bet that the experience is not going to get better after you buy. That's going to be the same amount of effort that he puts into your bill issues, helping you understand something about your phone, or filing a claim when you need him most.

In contrast, if you interact with someone that stood before you even opened the door, that's positive, upbeat, confident about their product and pricing, makes great eye contact, and is focused on you, what's your level of buy-in? Is this somebody that you could see yourself buying from? Absolutely. It's the four elements of communication that created that perception.

THE FOUR ELEMENTS OF COMMUNICATION

SPOKEN WORDS

In sales, your goal is to deliver clarity in a persuasive manner using all four forms of communication effectively. To start, it's important that we carefully select the words we choose. Our words carry weight. How we deliver those words is equally important, if not more important, but when crafting a delivery, it's a smoother process to build the nonverbal forms of communication around the verbal form.

When crafting your pitch, you should spend quality time selecting your words carefully for the following reasons:

Words create emotion. They have the power to evoke emotion, and emotions play a significant role in the decision-making process. Using the right words can create positive emotions in your customer, making them more likely to buy from you.
Words build trust. Using clear and concise language, demonstrating your expertise and knowledge, and showing empathy toward your customer's needs can help them trust you, your product or service, and your company.

Words convey value. When selling a product or service, it's important to communicate the value it provides. The words you choose can help convey the value of what you're selling and why it's worth the investment.

Words differentiate. In a competitive marketplace, the words you use can help differentiate your product or service from others. Using unique language to describe what you offer can help your customer understand how your product or service is different and why it's better.

Words persuade. Finally, the words you use can be persuasive. By understanding your customer's needs and using language that resonates with them, you can persuade them to make a decision that is in your favor.

Ultimately, the words you use in sales can make a significant impact on your ability to close deals and build long-lasting relationships. By choosing your words carefully and using language that resonates with the person you're communicating with, you can significantly increase your results.

Let's take a look at a script example, analyze it together, and break it down better understand the 'why' behind the word selection of the script.

Let's say a wireless consultant named Vince has a customer enter their store wanting to know the difference between them and competing carriers.

"So, Brian, great question. The primary advantages you're going to get with us over some of the other carriers are going to be, one, our network is insanely reliable, we have the most competitive device pricing in the industry, and we offer a 30-day 100% risk-free trial period because we have confidence in our value. So, I know you wanted to see what you qualified for, do you have your ID on you?" – Vince

Let's take a look at the word choice.

The very first thing Vince did was use the customer's name. The legendary Dale Carnegie said, *"A person's name is to him or her the sweetest and most important sound in any language."*[1] The customer feels valued and respected when you use their name in conversation. It also sends a message to the customer that you cared enough about them to remember it.

The next keyword that stood out to me is *"advantage"*. When the customer hears this, they think *"okay, this is the core value"*, and they're most likely to retain it because their goal is to compare it to others. When Vince listed out those advantages, he made sure that he highlighted the most valuable offers. That's why he chose network, pricing, and risk-free trial period in the example. Those are three things that customers really value – dependability of the network, pricing, and a risk-free trial period for superior peace of mind if they have any uncertainty.

Another important keyword that catches my attention is the word *"qualified"*. If you're in an industry where a customer must have their credit run to be approved, you should never use the words credit check. By definition, *"credit check"* and *"qualify"* are nearly identical. However, words have feelings behind them, or connotations. The term credit check does not bring about positive feelings. *"Qualify"* on the other hand, has a positive, or at the very least, a more neutral connotation.

Considering we cannot see or hear the script, we can't evaluate the articulation, tonality, and body language, but the script does leave some clues. Because of how well-crafted the script is, we can gather that this associate likely has a lot of confidence and certainty in his voice, allowing him to pronounce his words clearly with a friendly cadence. This delivery allows the customer to actually understand the information so they can make an educated decision.

As a buyer, I'm going to have more confidence in someone that delivers the information I need in a well-articulated manner.

ARTICULATION

In sales, clear and effective communication is paramount. When you articulate your message well, you establish credibility, build trust, and make it easy for your customers to understand the value of your product or service. In contrast, poor articulation can lead to confusion, misunderstandings, and lost sales opportunities.

ARTICULATION: MASTERING

Annihilate Ambiguity with proper enunciation and pronunciation. Don't let sloppy speech sabotage your sales. Nail your enunciation and pronunciation to command attention and make every word count. Train like a sales warrior by reading aloud and focusing on each syllable. Embrace the challenge and watch your sales game soar.

Set the Pace: Deliver Rhythm that Sells. You're not in this business to be dull. Keep your audience captivated with a well-paced rhythm that gives them time to digest your message. Use pauses to drive home crucial points and show them who's in charge.

Deliver clarity, and abandon complexity. Your customers don't have time for confusing jargon. Deliver laser-focused messages with simplicity and precision. Cut through the noise and watch your sales figures skyrocket.

Silence your verbal fillers. Verbal fillers, such as "um," "like," and "you know," can detract from your message and make you appear less confident. To eliminate these fillers, practice speaking slowly and thoughtfully. When you feel the urge to use a filler, pause instead. The more you practice, the easier it becomes to avoid these verbal crutches.

TONALITY

An entire chapter can be dedicated to tonality because it's one of the most fundamental elements that go into selling and building rapport. It's where your personality really shines through.

Just like words, the tone of your voice has the power to evoke emotion. Using the right tonality can create a positive emotional response in your customer, making them more likely to trust you and be receptive to what you're saying.

Your tone can also convey your level of confidence in what you're selling. If you speak with conviction and enthusiasm, your customer is more likely to believe in what you're selling. Coupling this with a friendly and approachable tone, you can create a sense of trust and likability with your customer.

Though, one of the most powerful effects of properly used tonality is delivering empathy. When a salesperson is able to understand and empathize with a customer's needs, concerns, and motivations, they are better able to communicate the value of their product or service in a way that resonates with the customer. This allows the salesperson to create a more positive and personalized experience for the customer, which can lead to greater satisfaction and loyalty.

All of these elements of tonality allow you to create excitement about your product, service, or idea. By speaking with enthusiasm, conviction, and empathy, you transfer that energy.

TONALITY: MASTERING

The key to great tonality in sales is ultimately authenticity. Your tonality should match the message you're trying to convey and come across as genuine and sincere. Here are a few tips for mastering tonality:

Use a natural tone. Speak in a natural tone of voice that feels comfortable for you. Avoid trying to sound like someone else or forcing a tone that doesn't feel authentic.

Match your tone to the message. Your tone should match the message you're trying to convey. If you're talking about a serious topic, your tone should be serious. If you're trying to create excitement, your tone should be enthusiastic.

Speak clearly and confidently. Speaking clearly and confidently can help you convey your message effectively. Avoid speaking too quickly or softly, which can make it difficult for your customer to understand you.

Listen actively. Great tonality also involves active listening. Pay attention to your customer's tone and adjust your tone accordingly to create a sense of rapport and understanding.

Show empathy. Use a caring and empathetic tone to show your customer that you understand their needs and are there to help them find a solution.

Practice. Most importantly, practicing your tonality can help you refine your skills and feel more confident in your sales approach. Record yourself speaking and listen back to identify areas where you can improve.

Use these tips as a blueprint for mastering your tone for optimal results. As you continue to polish your tonality, encourage feedback from others, record yourself, and continually fine-tune until you can feel the authenticity in your voice.

BODY LANGUAGE

Body language is arguably the most important of the four forms of communication. This is because our body language tells a more truthful story than our words do. Your words can say you care, but your body language could say otherwise.

When mastering body language, there are a few critical areas you want to focus on.

Maintain eye contact. Making great eye contact shows that you're engaged and interested in what the other person has to say. It also conveys confidence and credibility.

Defining "great" eye contact is easier said than done because there has to be a balance. Too much eye contact and you come off as too pushy or just creepy.

If you have too little eye contact or are shifty-eyed, you appear unsure of yourself or untrustworthy. A good rule of thumb is you want to make eye contact about 60% of the time when you're speaking and just a little more when you're listening – somewhere around 70%.[2]

Some of the most important times to make sure you're making eye contact are when you're explaining key points and asking questions. So if you were to ask *"Is there any reason you wouldn't want to get this in motion?"*, how well do they connect with you if you're staring at their feet?

Use open gestures. Open gestures, such as uncrossed arms and legs, show that you're open and receptive. This can help build trust and make them feel more comfortable.

Make use of hand gestures. The use of hand gestures does wonders for your charisma by bringing your words to life. This helps establish you as someone who's energetic, warm, and overall trustworthy. Think of hand gestures as underlining, bolding, italicizing your spoken words, or creating a visual picture for your listener. For example, a common gesture I use is having each hand represent two different things to create greater separation visually when I'm referring to the thing that I have assigned to each hand.

Lean in. Slightly leaning in toward whom you're listening to can show that you're interested in what they have to say and can create a sense of intimacy.

Mirror body language. This can help create a sense of rapport and understanding. However, be careful not to overdo it, as it can come across as insincere and intentional, resulting in a more damaging effect.

Avoid fidgeting. Fidgeting, such as tapping your foot or playing with a pen, can be distracting and make you seem nervous or uninterested. When I see someone tapping their pen on the table, I don't hear a single they're saying. I'm just focused on their fidgeting.

Have a genuine smile. Smiling can help create a positive and friendly atmosphere, which can help put anyone at ease. Everyone loves a good smile, and for good scientific reason. Research has shown that when we see someone else smile, it triggers the release of certain brain chemicals (such as dopamine, serotonin, and endorphins) that make us feel good. This can cause us to smile in return, even if we weren't feeling particularly happy or cheerful beforehand.[3]

Be aware of personal space. Be mindful of the other person's personal space and avoid invading it. This can make them feel uncomfortable and create a negative impression, or even lead to them feeling like you're trying to intimidate them. It can also be disastrous for anyone that's on the receiving end of bad breath.

A lot of times, we send messages when we communicate that we're not even aware of because we don't think about the impact of the word choice, articulation, tonality, and body language. Communication is one of the most important skills we possess as human beings, and it's at the heart of our success. It is the process of exchanging information and ideas between individuals, groups, and organizations that, also, just happen to be the gatekeeping element to your success. On your path to disruptive performance, it's insanely important to pour a great amount of time and energy into your communication skills by keeping these four elements of communication in mind.

When we communicate, we transmit energy. If you have to speak to get your job done, understand that you are contagious. Unlike a virus though, you have full control over what you transmit. That transmission will be a reflection of your emotional state and delivery in your communication.

For example, if you have a shaken belief in your product, service, or idea, if you doubt the value and present them unenthusiastically, you're transmitting those feelings of uncertainty, doubt, and dullness. In contrast, if you bring out the best versions of the four elements of communication, you transmit those same feelings of certainty, excitement, trust, and authenticity.

CHAPTER 6

STARTING FROM ZERO – THE 100-SHOT SHAKEUP

The secret to starting from zero isn't so secret. It's simply to get started. The real secret is in the strategies and discipline to stay the course. In this chapter, I'll share my number one top-performing customer approach that you can use to literally stop any bypassing customer, build a relationship within that window of opportunity, and go in for the appointment set, or even the close.

If you've ever worked in a mall environment, you know that unless you're an expert, it comes with a great deal of challenges and can be intimidating at first. And even a lot of top performers still struggle with it. They might perform better in a different environment that doesn't require that kind of outreach. But I'm going to give you the best approach to develop the skillset needed to outperform anyone in any environment. And with that, I want to introduce you to something I call the 100-shot shakeup.

It's an exercise that I require new employees to carry out to get them out of their comfort zone. The idea is simple – you have to approach 100 people a day face-to-face until you have a thirst for rejection. For the setting, you can be anywhere – a mall, a strip center, a stand-alone store, a park, a festival – doesn't matter. This challenge is designed purely with the intention to get comfortable with rejection. Why? It's because that's where growth takes place.

You see, challenges, setbacks, and rejections are inherent to the process of selling. Developing a thick layer of comfortability for rejection makes salespeople more resilient. It helps develop an eye for identifying when it's time to move to the next opportunity. It allows confidence to permeate throughout their process because they've been desensitized by the rejection.

Top performers use rejection in two ways. One, we take the rejection on as a challenge. Ultimately, we just want to see if we can overcome it. That's that go-get-it mindset that's woven in and out of our very being. Two, we see it as an opportunity to enhance our approach. Maybe this one customer had a uniquely valid objection that we hadn't thought of or planned for. Uncovering new objections from customers empowers salespeople to refine their strategies to develop tailored solutions. This bolsters their arsenal, allowing them to tackle similar concerns and close deals with future customers more effectively.

THE G.R.E.A.T. PROCESS

Before we dive headfirst into the challenge, I want to introduce you to a framework I adopted early on in my sales career that, after a couple of injections of wit and sales strategy personalization, revolutionized and streamlined my sales training as a leader. It created an efficient and effective fast-track method that was greatly responsible for accelerating our growth as a wireless franchise. It all began when nTelos Wireless (eventually acquired by Sprint and later merged with T-Mobile) introduced the G.R.E.A.T. Process[1]. It's as followed:

Greet: The introduction stage. Begin the interaction by introducing yourself to the potential customer. A genuine smile and a dash of charm can set the stage for a positive and engaging conversation.

Relationship: The rapport-building & inquisitive stage. Capture their name, as well as pets, children, spouse, or anyone else around to make the interaction more personable. This is also where you'll ask intentional questions, getting to know the prospects' problems and what sort of solution they're looking for.

Educate: The value-building stage. Once you established rapport, you educate them on the solution to their problem. This contains who you are, the company, the product or service benefits, warranties, FAQs, etc. Have a clear and concise, yet comprehensive, approach.

Note: For the 100-shot challenge, we're going minimalist, only sharing the high-value bullet points. These highlighted points will pique the potential customer's interest if you have any shot at all to convert them into a lead or a sale.

Ask: The Call-To-Action stage. Guide the prospect toward the next step in the sales process. This could involve checking if they qualify for a special offer, inviting them to visit your store, or setting up an appointment for a more in-depth discussion.

Thank: The appreciation stage. As you wrap up the interaction, it's crucial to show appreciation for the time and effort the potential customer has invested in the conversation. Express gratitude for their attention, engagement, and patience throughout the process. If a sale is made, don't forget to congratulate them on their excellent decision and welcome them to your customer family. In addition, use this stage to present any referral incentives, loyalty programs, or follow-up opportunities that may be relevant to the prospect. Let them know that their satisfaction is your priority and that you're always available for any questions, concerns, or assistance they may need in the future. This final step not only leaves a lasting positive impression but also paves the way for a long-term, mutually beneficial relationship with your new customer.

THE 100 SHOT SHAKEUP CHALLENGE

Before you review the steps below, be mindful that you will not master The Creator role from behind the cash wrap or from your desk waiting for a customer to appear. Disrupt your comfort level and step into the place where real results happen. Even if you have a lead source or don't necessarily deal with customers directly, you will only enhance your skillset by acquiring this skill to look rejection in the face and push to the next opportunity without a loss of enthusiasm or confidence.

The Steps

Step 1: Show up wherever you plan to carry out the challenge.

Step 2: Greet the first person in sight with a handshake while following the G.R.E.A.T. process.

For the example script, we'll customize it for a solar consultant attempting to generate leads.

SCRIPT:

Consultant: *"Hey! I just want to introduce myself, my name is <name> and I work for <your company>. What's your name?"*

Lead: *"John"*

Pro tip: If you see something relatable, incorporate it here! For example, if the customer is wearing an NFL hat that you're a fan of or even despise, inject some charm by making a friendly joke about the team.

Consultant: *"Are you a homeowner, by chance?"*

Lead: *"Yep!"*

Consultant: *"Well listen, John, I'll keep it short. What I do is help homeowners take control of their power and save money with no down payment or any kind of up-front out-of-pocket expense. We've already helped around 5,000 customers in this state own their power, and we're ranked as the #1 solar company here. If I* *could save you money so you can kick the power company to the curb, would there be any reason you wouldn't want to at least learn more about how solar works?"*

Lead: *"No, I've actually been hearing about it, just never looked into it."*

Consultant: *"If your home qualifies, it really makes sense 10x out of 10. It's my job to really just give you all of the info you need to make an educated decision one way or the other. What day and time works best for you this week to connect?"*

Lead: *"Let's shoot for Saturday at 1"*

Consultant: *"Got it! Thank you, John! I'll give you a shout the day of just to confirm."*

Step 3: Repeat!

That's it!

Consider the impact this single activity can do for your personal growth and income. The more you step out of your comfort zone, the more you will expand your comfort zone. Over time, what was once daunting or frightening transforms into familiar territory and becomes more comfortable.

Even if you're in leadership and not working directly with customers, you can leverage this to challenge to recruit or train your team to generate leads. Think of the perception your team starts to develop when they see their leader step up and take massive action and seizing the initiative.

If you're looking for actionable content, this single exercise is one of the most powerful practices that you can carry out immediately to help elevate your skillset. So I challenge you – take on the 100-shot shakeup. If you want to be the creator of your own opportunities, you have to be willing to roll up your sleeves and get to work.

They say that you miss 100% of the shots you don't take. Do you want to warm the bench and watch somebody else take the shot? Or do you want to jump into the game and dominate?

CHAPTER 7

OPPORTUNITY OPTIMIZATION

In sales, the worst thing you can do is not close. The second worse thing you can do is to not maximize the sales when you do close.

Even the most passionate business owners can be upside down quickly without a keen sense of upselling and the effects it has on their bottom line. If you decided to open a coffee shop without understanding the power of maximizing your revenue opportunity, your passion can drive you out of business.

This is why you might see revenue-driven coffee shops training their baristas to offer an extra shot of espresso or a pastry at checkout.

When you have a shop that serves 5,000 coffee drinks a month with zero extra shot upsells, that's $1,000 created overnight in additional revenue with a 20% attachment rate and $1 per extra shot. That single best practice that took no additional resources to create could cover the rent!

When you tweak the practices to have a more revenue-driven approach, the results shine through.

The formula is simple:
You ask > you highlight a value point, if needed > you close.

That's it. I know, it's profound, right? Luckily, you don't have to be profound to get top-performer results, you just have to have *"a little bit of give a damn"*, in the famous words of Darrell Turner.

Because, believe it or not, 90% of the success of this formula is out of the very first component - ask. That's the number one reason salespeople never reach their greatest potential. They don't present the idea. They're not present. They don't show up for the opportunity.

So if you want to make an immediate improvement in your sales results - simply present whatever that additional offer is.

That very best practice won me over today. Waiting on my vehicle to have its oil changed, I walked across the parking lot to Burger King to grab a quick bite. As I ordered my chicken sandwich, the cashier asked if I'd like to add two baked cookies. *"They just came out!"*, she said. I had zero intentions of getting any sweets, but I'm a sucker for a good dessert. Because she offered, it triggered my sweet tooth. I sighed and said, *"why did you have to ask?"*. Needless to say, I added the cookies to my order.

When you analyze some of the most successful companies in the world, they all share a common theme: maximize every opportunity.

Spotify: Upgrade to their premium account for an ad-free experience.[1]

Apple: Asked to purchase additional accessories, such as cases, headphones, or chargers.[2]

McDonald's: *"Would you like to make that a combo?"*[3]

Success leaves clues. If want to take your revenue to the next level, all you have to do is follow the methods the most successful companies use.

Here are 11 proven ways to start adding to your revenue immediately:

1. SUGGEST COMPLEMENTARY PRODUCTS OR SERVICES

For example: if a customer is buying a camera, you could suggest a tripod or an extra lens to go with it.

As soon as you add a product to your Amazon cart, you get a dozen windows beneath. "This is often purchased with", "Add the best selling <product> to your order", "Recommended based on your shopping trends"[4], "Inspired by your browsing history", and the list goes on. According to Forbes, Amazon attributes up to 35% of its revenue to these suggestions alone![5]

2. OFFER A HIGHER-END VERSION OF THE PRODUCT

For example: if a customer is interested in a basic laptop, you could suggest a more powerful model with better features. Every large plane has its first-class cabin and every 5-star hotel has its suites for a reason. Many customers want the best experience, not the most affordable.

3. PROVIDE BUNDLE DEALS

For example: if a customer is buying a phone, you could offer a deal that includes a phone case and screen protector at a discounted price if bundled together.

As we collected data from our upsell offers, we found it was best to have multiple options to extend. We would have two core offers – a free tablet add-on that just required the service fee and a bundled protection offer that included liquid glass and a case. Top-performing locations would achieve a 50% attachment rate on tablets alone for every new customer account created just by making it a disciplined behavior on every single customer interaction.

4. OFFER LOYALTY PROGRAMS

For example: have an app or physical punchcard that users can keep to earn points for redeeming a free or discounted product or service.

You've probably experienced these daily from CVS's ExtraCare[6] to Starbucks Rewards[7]. Having a loyalty program is an effective way to earn repeat business, increase spending and collect data to gain insight into their customers' purchases and preferences for enhancing marketing and sales strategies.

5. PROVIDE LIMITED-TIME OFFERS

For example: If you have older inventory to move, you can offer a flash sale on your product or service.

This offer creates a sense of urgency and incentivizes the customer to take action before the sale is over or inventory is depleted.

6. SUGGEST A MAINTENANCE OR SERVICE PLAN

For example: If you own a lawn care business, you can provide ongoing services such as fertilization, weed control, or even spray painting their lawn during winter months.

This offer creates a residual element to your revenue that can overcome the challenges that can come with a seasonal industry.

7. PROMOTE AN EXCLUSIVE OR LIMITED EDITION ITEM

For example: This could be a unique shirt design that is only released to its followers that are part of a social media group or have downloaded the company app.

Golden Goose is always releasing app-exclusive shoe designs[8]. This not only increases sales in the short term but continues to create a strong sense of community with its followers.

8. SUGGEST A GIFT CARD FOR FUTURE USE

A simple display can make an easy last-minute gift into a long-lasting revenue driver. Gift cards can help businesses increase brand awareness and attract new customers. When customers give a gift card to someone else, they are essentially endorsing the business and introducing it to a new potential customer. And there is no better way to recommend your business than to have your existing customers do it for you.

9. SUGGEST A CUSTOM OR PERSONALIZED OPTION

For example: If you sell physical products, you could add custom engravings to the products to personalize the experience.

10. OFFER A MEMBERSHIP OR SUBSCRIPTION PLAN

While this structure is usually found to be the primary monetization model of a business, it isn't always. You can use membership as a secondary source of revenue. LinkedIn Premium[9], for example. At the time of writing, LinkedIn reports having around 900 million users, with roughly 39% paying for the premium subscription-based features.[10]

11. SHARE BUY ONE GET ONE PROMOTION (BOGO)

> This is a favorite of mine from the wireless days. If we had a customer enter that had an odd number of phones that was looking to upgrade or switch from another carrier, we trained our team to always throw out any BOGO offers to convert three accounts into four. This always hit home when the parents had a younger child they weren't quite ready to get a phone for, but the free device was incentive enough to get it early. And when we bundled this with the free tablet offer, those three-line accounts quickly converted to five-line accounts.

There are thousands of studies that demonstrate that upselling can have a significant impact on a company's revenue, customer lifetime value, customer retention rates, and overall success. By offering relevant and personalized upsells, companies can increase customer satisfaction, loyalty, and engagement, while also generating additional revenue. Millions of dollars have been spent collecting, analyzing, and implementing these up-sell strategies to drive substantial revenue into the business. You can capitalize on those efforts for free just by following the data. Which strategies do you plan to implement?

PART 3

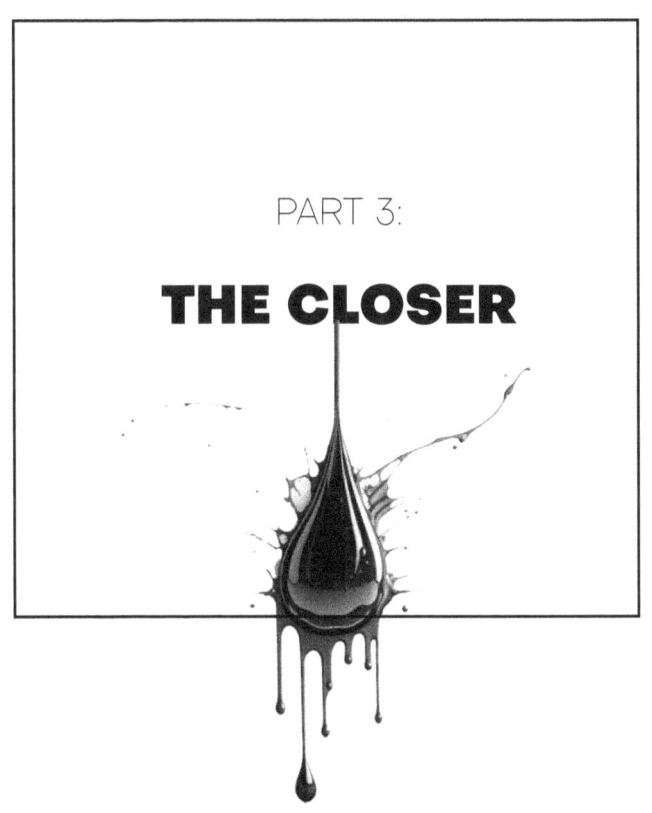

PART 3:

THE CLOSER

CHAPTER 8

CLOSERS RULEBOOK: 10 CLOSER COMMANDMENTS

What makes a great closer? Is it the ability to communicate effectively? The persistence in follow-up? Their goal-oriented nature? Their sheer confidence? Or maybe their creative problem-solving skills to navigate through the objections on their way to the yes? While these traits greatly contribute to the success of a closer, there's one simple rule you should follow no matter what: **never walk away from a customer without asking for their business.** Results are simply in the ask. Even if you stumble throughout the process, asking for the business can yield more sales than a highly polished seller who fails to ask.

There's nothing more frustrating than to witness a talented communicator sell the hell out of a product or service and leave empty-handed because they neglected to ask for the business. It's like watching a skilled fisherman prepare the line, hook a fish, watch the ripple in the water swirl around, and fail to even attempt to reel it in.

A closer's only job is to convert leads into profitable deals. So, if you're not asking, you're just practicing.

Now, if it were only that simple, we could end the chapter here. As you might've guessed, that's not quite the case. That's why I've written the 10 indispensable closer commandments designed to arm you with the essential principles that set apart the sales elite from the rest. Here, we delve into the commandments that will elevate your sales prowess, providing you with the fundamental knowledge and tools to consistently close deals and achieve disruptive sales results.

With each commandment you internalize, you will achieve a new level of sales expertise, equipping yourself with the tools and insights to excel in the sales landscape with utmost confidence and unparalleled success.

Keep in mind, as you embark on this educational journey, that the secret to true mastery resides not just in comprehending these commandments but in consistently embodying them in your daily practice. Embrace the knowledge contained within this chapter, and witness your sales proficiency ascend to unprecedented heights. The journey commences now.

10 CLOSER COMMANDMENTS

COMMANDMENT 1:
THOU SHALT SET PROPER EXPECTATIONS

Honor thy sales process by first setting forth proper expectations, as they are the pillars upon which fruits are exalted.

Architects and engineers face a multitude of challenges when designing and constructing mega-tall structures. They must take into account several factors, such as the building's ability to withstand earthquakes, wind resistance, and other environmental forces. As these structures reach for the sky, the demands placed on them increase, necessitating innovative and robust design solutions.

Among the myriad of considerations, the foundation is of paramount importance. Foundations for these cloud-kissing structures can reach depths of up to 85 meters or more. This is because the larger and taller the structure, the deeper and stronger the foundation must be to support the immense weight and stresses placed upon it. A well-engineered foundation ensures the building's stability and longevity, allowing it to stand tall and withstand various external forces.

This principle can be applied to the sales process. Just as the foundation is crucial to the success and integrity of a mega-tall structure, setting clear and strong expectations with potential customers is critical for achieving fruitful results when closing a sale. The deeper and more robust the foundation of expectations, the more likely it is that the sales relationship will withstand challenges and thrive.

By setting proper expectations from the beginning, you create a stable base for the sales process to build upon. This foundation fosters trust and understanding between the salesperson and the potential client, enabling the relationship to weather any uncertainties or obstacles that may arise. Moreover, it allows the salesperson to navigate the sales process more effectively, ultimately increasing the likelihood of securing a successful close.

The importance of a strong foundation in both mega-tall structures and the sales process cannot be understated. By understanding the parallel between these two seemingly unrelated fields, you can apply the principles of engineering and architecture to your approach, ensuring you lay the groundwork for a successful close. Here are a few best practices to be mindful of when crafting your expectations:

CRYSTAL CLEAR COMMUNICATION

No one likes a salesperson who conceals information. Setting proper expectations means communicating clearly and honestly with your customers. Be upfront about what they can expect from your product or service, and don't sugarcoat the facts or make promises you can't keep. Remember, transparency is always the best policy - and it's a surefire way to earn your customers' trust and respect.

THE ART OF MANAGING EXPECTATIONS — IT'S ALL ABOUT BALANCE

Setting proper expectations is a delicate balancing act. You're a tightrope walker juggling torches while reciting Shakespeare. On one hand, you want to highlight the benefits and value of your offering; on the other, you don't want to oversell and underdeliver. The key is to find the sweet spot between the two. Be realistic, but also emphasize the unique selling points that set you apart from the competition. Your potential customers will appreciate your candor, and you'll be well on your way to closing those deals.

EXPECTATION VS. REALITY: JUST KEEP IT REAL.

We've all been victims: you buy something based on its dazzling marketing claims, only to be bitterly disappointed when it fails to live up to the hype. As a closer, your job is to ensure your customers don't experience that same crushing sense of disillusionment. By setting proper expectations and being honest about what your product or service can deliver, you'll help bridge the gap between expectation and reality - and keep your customers coming back for more.

THE RIPPLE EFFECT: WORD-OF-MOUTH ADVERTISING AT ITS FINEST

When you set proper expectations and deliver on your promises, something magical happens: your customers become your biggest fans. Word-of-mouth advertising is the most powerful and cost-effective marketing tool out there, and it all starts with setting proper expectations. So, do yourself a favor: lay the groundwork for a legion of loyal customers who'll sing your praises from the rooftops. Trust me, your bottom line will thank you.

THE LONG GAME: CULTIVATING LASTING RELATIONSHIPS

In the world of sales, it's all too easy to get caught up in the thrill of the chase and forget about the bigger picture. The most successful salespeople know that the real gold is in cultivating lasting relationships with their customers. By setting proper expectations from the outset, you'll not only increase your chances of closing the deal but also lay the groundwork for a long-term partnership based on trust, respect, and mutual benefit. And that is the ultimate sales victory.

In conclusion, take this commandment to heart, and make it your mission to weave it into the very fabric of your sales approach.

COMMANDMENT 2:
THOU SHALT CUT THE FLUFF

Speaketh with simplistic clarity and precision, discarding unnecessary jargon and excessive details.

Selling with simple, clear, and concise language is like making the perfect grilled cheese sandwich - no fuss, just the right ingredients, and absolutely satisfying. Many salespeople mistakenly believe that they need to throw glitter on their language or borrow terms from product manuals to win customers. But unless you're talking to a tech guru, it's best to save that expert lingo for Reddit. Overdoing it with technical jargon, being pretentious, or even trying to be too charming can distract from what really matters - clear, concise, and simple communication.

Spewing technical terms in a sales pitch is like trying to impress a date with a pocket full of magic tricks - it's awkward and misses the point. Focus on being clear, brief, and genuine in your sales approach, and sprinkle your conversations with humor and wit. By doing so, you'll see better results in your sales performance and truly embody the spirit of a top sales leader.

As a general rule, if a five-year-old can't understand your explanation, your delivery is too complicated.

In the realm of sales, time is more than just a fleeting resource; it is the very lifeblood of success. Every word that escapes your lips, every slide in your presentation, and every moment spent with your prospect should be carefully crafted to serve the ultimate goal: closing the deal. The key to unlocking a higher success rate in this endeavor is to cut out the fluff, eliminate distractions, and optimize your sales pitch to be as streamlined and effective as a well-honed blade. In short, the sharper the knife, the cleaner the cut.

Picture yourself as a master chef preparing a gourmet meal. Your ingredients are your prospects' needs, your cooking skills represent your sales expertise, and the garnish on the plate signifies the added value you bring to the table. However, if you were to smother the dish with excessive sauce, the diner would be unable to savor the true essence of the meal. The same is true in sales; when you cloud your pitch with superfluous details, jargon, and unnecessary anecdotes, you dilute the potency of your message.

Consider two salespeople, Alex and Ava. Both were tasked with selling the same innovative software solution. Alex, a loquacious fellow, believed that the more he spoke, the more impressive he would sound. He would go into painstaking detail about every feature, overwhelming his prospects with jargon-infused monologues. At the end of his sales pitch, prospects were often left dazed, confused, and hesitant to commit.

Ava, on the other hand, understood the power of clarity. She tailored her pitch to focus solely on the specific pain points her prospects faced and demonstrated how her software could alleviate their troubles. Ava spoke in plain language, using concise examples and relatable analogies that resonated with her audience. By the time she reached the close, her prospects felt understood, informed, and eager to take action.

In this example, Ava triumphed because she knew that the key to unlocking her prospects' hearts and wallets was to eliminate distractions and focus on the core of their needs. She presented her solution in a manner that was simple, digestible, and easy to understand. The result? Ava enjoyed a significantly higher success rate and closed more deals than her verbose counterpart, Alex.

Moreover, by cutting the fluff and optimizing your sales pitch, you not only increase your chances of closing the deal at hand but also free up valuable time to pursue additional opportunities. Sales is a numbers game, and every minute spent over-explaining or indulging in tangents with a prospect who may not even be a buyer is a minute lost to engage with a potential customer who could be eager to sign on the dotted line.

As if I plucked from your mother's guiltiest soap opera pleasure, "Time, akin to grains in an hourglass, spares no one." It is your responsibility as a sales professional to make every moment count. By cutting out the fluff, keeping your pitch focused and straightforward, and maximizing the value of each interaction, you will optimize your sales process and close at a higher success rate. Remember, the realm of sales is not a theater for verbosity; it's an arena for being comprehensively concise and to the point.

COMMAND 3:

THOU SHALT MASTER THE ART OF LISTENING

Hone thy listening skills, truly understanding the needs, desires, and concerns of thy prospects.

it's easy to get caught up in the adrenaline-fueled race to close deals and become the sales champion we all strive to be. However, a true secret weapon of a master closer isn't the flashiest presentation or the slickest pitch–it's the power of listening. That's right, mate, one of the most lethal tools in your arsenal is none other than your ears.

You see, when we engage in conversation with a potential customer or client, our natural instinct is to dominate the discussion with our knowledge, charm, and wit. But I would urge you to pump the brakes and take a step back. Why? Because genuine, empathetic listening allows you to truly understand your prospects' needs, concerns, and desires. And once you've unlocked that treasure trove of insight, you can tailor your approach to create a solution that feels as if it was crafted just for them.

BOOMERANG TECHNIQUE

Imagine this scenario: You're at a party, and you meet someone new. In the midst of your conversation, they spend the entire time talking about themselves, barely allowing you to get a word in edgewise. How likely are you to want to continue the interaction? Not very, right? Now, consider the reverse: You're talking to someone who listens intently, asks thoughtful questions, and demonstrates genuine interest in what you have to say. Suddenly, you find yourself drawn to this person, and participating in conversational ping pong.

The same principle applies to sales and operates in this boomerang-styled effect. By throwing out open-ended questions and allowing your prospect to share their story, you create an opportunity for valuable information to be returned. And when it's time for you to share your solution, you can skillfully weave in the nuggets of data you've extracted from your prospect, making your offering resonate on a deeper, more personal level. Boom. Boomerang skills are in full swing.

But the power of listening doesn't stop there. By genuinely tuning into your prospects' concerns and objections, you can address them with empathy and understanding. This demonstrates that you're not just another salesperson trying to make a quick dollar; you're a trusted advisor who cares about their well-being and is dedicated to finding a solution that truly meets their needs.

So how do you become a master listener? It's simple: quiet your mind, focus on your prospect, and let curiosity guide you. Ask open-ended questions, and resist the urge to interrupt or interject with your own thoughts. Remember, the more you learn about your prospect, the better equipped you'll be to close the deal.

In conclusion, it's time we all take a moment to appreciate the unsung hero of sales success: the art of listening. By embracing the power of empathetic, genuine listening, you'll not only close more deals but also forge stronger, more meaningful relationships with your clients. And in the end, that's another commandment that truly separates the average salesperson from the extraordinary closer.

COMMANDMENT 4:
THOU SHALT ASK GREAT QUESTIONS

Engage thy prospects with insightful inquiries, unveiling their motivations and guiding them toward thy offering.

In the high-octane world of sales, the pursuit of closing deals and hitting quotas can often feel like a complex dance. However, we have yet again another power weapon: the power of asking great questions. The key to unlocking the hidden potential of any sales interaction lies in the thoughtful inquiries you make of your potential customers or clients.

In sales, the right questions are the keys to the kingdom, unlocking the gates to your prospect's mind and heart. So, how do you use this powerful tool to close more deals? By crafting questions that cut through the noise and get to the core of your prospect's needs, fears, and aspirations. Great questions not only uncover invaluable information but also serve to build rapport, trust, and credibility.

QUESTIONS THAT REIGN SUPREME

Here are five examples of insightful questions that you might ask to guide a prospect on their journey to a closed deal:

"If you could wave a magic wand and solve one problem in your business, what would it be?"
This question dives deep into your prospect's pain points and helps identify the areas where your solution can make the greatest impact.

"What does success look like to you, both personally and professionally?"

Understanding your prospect's definition of success allows you to align your offering with their long-term goals and demonstrate the value of your solution in the context of their bigger picture.

"What are the challenges or obstacles that you foresee in achieving your desired outcome?"

By uncovering potential roadblocks, you can proactively address concerns and demonstrate your commitment to helping your prospect overcome any hurdles they may face.

"What have you tried in the past to address this issue, and what were the results?"

This question sheds light on your prospect's previous experiences and can help you differentiate your offering from other solutions they may have tried.

"If we were to work together, what would be the most critical factor in ensuring a successful partnership?"

By asking your prospect to define the key elements of a successful collaboration, you can tailor your approach to meet their expectations and create a winning partnership.

Asking insightful questions is a skill that requires practice and finesse. It's not just about the questions themselves, but also about the timing, delivery, and follow-up. When engaging with a potential customer or client, pay close attention to their responses, adapt your approach accordingly, and don't be afraid to ask follow-up questions that delve deeper into the heart of the matter.

In conclusion, the art of asking great questions is a cornerstone of sales success, and mastering this skill can set you apart from the competition. By crafting thought-provoking inquiries that resonate with your prospects, you'll not only uncover invaluable information but also build deeper relationships that ultimately result in a higher number of successful deals. So, the next time you find yourself in the throes of a sales conversation, remember this: The most potent potion for sales success lies not in the answers you provide, but in the questions that you ask.

COMMAND 5:

THOU SHALT BE A STORYTELLING WIZARD

Enthrall thy prospects with captivating tales, evoking emotions and illuminating the benefits of thy solution.

As you can see, there are many techniques and tactics that salespeople employ in their quest to close deals and conquer quotas. Yet, there's one strategy that stands head and shoulders above some - the power of storytelling.

A sales pitch without storytelling is like a burger without the sauce - it's bland, forgettable, and unlikely to hit the spot. So, how do you infuse your sales pitch with the magic of storytelling?

Here are the key ingredients to crafting a persuasive narrative that resonates with your audience:

KNOW YOUR AUDIENCE

Before you can craft a relatable story, you must first understand your prospect's unique experiences, challenges, and aspirations. Take the time to research your potential customer or client, and tailor your narrative to address their specific needs and concerns. By demonstrating that you've taken the time to understand their world, you'll forge a deeper connection and make your pitch more persuasive.

Set the stage with context

A powerful story begins with a compelling introduction that sets the stage for the narrative to unfold. In the context of a sales pitch, this means providing a clear overview of the problem or challenge your prospect is facing and creating a sense of urgency for finding a solution. By establishing the stakes early on, you'll pique your audience's interest and create a sense of anticipation for the story to come.

INTRODUCE RELATABLE CHARACTERS

The most memorable stories feature characters that resonate with the audience on a personal level. When crafting your narrative, consider introducing characters that mirror your prospect's experiences and challenges. This could be a previous client who faced similar issues or even yourself, sharing your own journey and insights. By humanizing your story, you'll make it easier for your prospect to identify with the characters and envision themselves in their shoes.

CREATE AN EMOTIONAL ARC

A persuasive story is a rollercoaster ride of emotions that takes the audience on a journey of transformation. To create an emotional arc in your narrative, consider incorporating elements of tension, conflict, and resolution that mirror the emotional journey your prospect may be experiencing. By tapping into their fears, hopes, and aspirations, you'll make your pitch more emotionally resonant and persuasive.

WEAVE IN SOCIAL PROOF

A concept coined by Robert Cialdini in his book Influence, social proof suggests that nothing speaks louder than the experiences of others who have walked the path before your prospect.[1] As you share your narrative, be sure to include real-life examples, testimonials, and case studies that demonstrate the effectiveness of your solution. By providing concrete evidence of success, you'll not only make your story more relatable but also bolster your credibility and trustworthiness.

BRING IT HOME WITH A CALL TO ACTION

A persuasive narrative culminates in a powerful call to action that encourages the audience to take the next step in their journey. As you draw your story to a close, make sure to include a clear, compelling, and relatable call to action that invites your prospect to join the ranks of your satisfied customers and clients.

USE RELATABLE ANALOGIES

A powerful storytelling technique is to use relatable analogies that make complex concepts easy to understand. By drawing parallels between your offering and familiar experiences or objects, you can help your prospect visualize the value of your solution in a way that resonates with their everyday lives. The simpler the analogy, the more powerful the connection.

MASTER THE ART OF PACING

In the world of storytelling, timing is everything. To keep your audience engaged and invested in your narrative, be mindful of the pacing of your sales pitch. Break up longer sections of content with anecdotes, examples, and questions to maintain interest and create a dynamic, conversational flow. A well-paced story is like a finely tuned symphony - each note perfectly timed to create a harmonious, unforgettable experience.

ADD A TOUCH OF HUMOR

Never underestimate the power of laughter to break down barriers and create rapport with your prospect. By infusing your narrative with a dash of wit and humor, you'll not only make your sales pitch more enjoyable but also foster a sense of camaraderie and trust. A good laugh is like a breath of fresh air in a stuffy boardroom - it clears the air and brings people together.

PRACTICE, PRACTICE, PRACTICE

Finally, as with any skill, mastering the art of storytelling takes time and practice. Regularly refine your narrative, solicit feedback from peers, and continuously hone your delivery. By investing in your storytelling skills, you'll not only become a more persuasive salesperson but also a more captivating communicator in all aspects of your life.

In conclusion, infusing your sales pitch with the magic of relatable storytelling can make your message more persuasive, engaging, and memorable. By crafting a narrative that resonates with your audience, humanizes your offering, and inspires action, you'll not only close more deals but also leave a lasting impression on the hearts and minds of your prospects. In the end, it's the stories we tell that make all the difference - so make yours a tale worth sharing.

COMMANDMENT 6:
THOU SHALT HONOR STRUCTURE

Equip thyself with extensive product knowledge, rehearsed presentations, tailored responses to possible objections, and a disciplined routine.

This tool, like many others, truly separates the good from the great - having a well-structured sales pitch and an equally well-structured routine. When it comes to becoming a disruptive closer, organization and preparation are the keys to success.

A well-structured sales pitch is like a perfectly choreographed dance - every step is deliberate, every move is intentional, and every beat is in perfect harmony. So, how do you master the art of structure in both your sales pitch and your daily routine? Dance with me.

KNOW YOUR SALES PITCH INSIDE OUT

To deliver a truly impactful sales pitch, you must know it like the back of your hand. This means memorizing your key talking points, anticipating common objections, and preparing responses that showcase the value of your offering. By committing your sales pitch to memory, you'll exude confidence, credibility, and professionalism - making it easier for your prospects to trust and invest in your solution. This also allows you to control your tone without thinking and your body language as a reinforced language, making the message explosively more effective.

DEVELOP A DAILY ROUTINE.

In the world of sales, consistency is king. By establishing a well-structured daily routine, you'll create the discipline and focus needed to achieve your goals. Begin by setting aside dedicated time each day for prospecting, following up, and closing deals. A day without structure is like a ship without a rudder - it drifts aimlessly and never reaches its destination.

PLAN YOUR WEEK

Just as a well-structured daily routine keeps you on track, a well-planned week ensures that you're always moving forward. Allocate time each week to review your progress, identify areas for improvement, and set clear, achievable goals for the days ahead. A well-planned week is like a roadmap to success - it shows you where you're going and helps you stay the course.

SET MONTHLY OBJECTIVES

It's essential to adopt a short-term perspective. By setting clear, achievable monthly objectives, you'll create a sense of direction and purpose that fuels your motivation and drive. I personally keep my goal-setting length to not extend beyond a month.

Have I had a checklist of things I want to achieve before I die, sure, but I've never set concrete long-term goals, and have never been an advocate. Why? When you're locked into a long-term plan, you might miss out on the gems hidden in plain sight - the opportunities that can change your life in an instant. A single thought can transform the trajectory of your life. One inspiring idea can ignite a fire in your soul and set you on a path that completely dissolves your five-year, meticulously thought-out plan.

By focusing on short and mid-term goals, usually, no longer than a month, or quarters at most, you give yourself the flexibility to seize those game-changing moments and capitalize on them.

CONTINUOUSLY REFINE AND IMPROVE

The world of sales is ever-evolving, and staying ahead of the curve requires constant growth and development. Make a commitment to continuously refine your sales pitch, hone your skills, and stay abreast of industry trends and best practices. In sales, the only constant is change - so embrace it, learn from it, and let it propel you forward.

MEASURE YOUR PROGRESS

To become an effective and efficient closer, it's crucial to track your performance and measure your progress against your goals. Regularly review your key performance indicators (KPIs), identify areas of success and areas that require improvement, and adjust your strategy and approach accordingly. What gets measured gets managed - and what gets managed gets results.

CELEBRATE YOUR SUCCESSES

Finally, never forget to acknowledge and celebrate your achievements - both big and small. By taking the time to recognize your victories, you'll cultivate a mindset of success and reinforce the habits and behaviors that drive results. In the end, it's the victories we celebrate that shape the story of our success - so make every win count.

COMMANDMENT 7:
THOU SHALT OPERATE WITH UNWAVERING INTEGRITY

Conduct thyself with honesty, transparency, and genuine concern for the well-being of thy prospects.

In the exhilarating world of sales, where dreams are made, and fortunes are won or lost at the drop of a hat, I've discovered a cornerstone of success that distinguishes the true champions from the flash-in-the-pan pretenders: integrity. The secret to sustained high performance lies in the noble art of operating with integrity.

But what does it mean to operate with integrity in sales? And how can embracing this virtue help you close more deals and build a lasting legacy of success?

TRUST

As I always say, "*Trust is the currency of sales - and integrity is the mint that creates it.*" Okay, maybe I've only said it once, and that was here, but it's true. By operating with integrity, you'll cultivate trust with your prospects, and that trust will translate into a more receptive audience for your sales pitch. After all, people do business with those they like and trust - and integrity is the foundation upon which these qualities are built.

REPUTATION

In the interconnected world we live in, your reputation can precede you - and in sales, a stellar reputation is worth its weight in gold. By conducting yourself with integrity, you'll create a brand that's synonymous with honesty, professionalism, and value. A reputation built on integrity is like a beacon that attracts the best clients, partners, and opportunities - so keep it shining bright.

LONG-TERM SUCCESS

In the race of sales, it's not the sprinters who win - it's the marathon runners who stay the course and play by the rules. While it may be tempting to cut corners or bend the rules to close a deal, the truth is that short-term gains often come at the expense of long-term success. By operating with integrity, you'll create a solid foundation for lasting achievement.

REPEAT BUSINESS AND REFERRALS

Operating with integrity not only helps you close deals but also encourages repeat business and referrals - two of the most valuable sources of revenue in sales. A happy customer is a walking billboard for your business - and a customer who trusts you is a customer who will come back for more.

PERSONAL GROWTH AND FULFILLMENT

Perhaps the most significant benefit of operating with integrity is the sense of personal growth and fulfillment it brings. By staying true to your values and always putting your clients' best interests first, you'll not only build a successful sales career but also cultivate a deep sense of pride and satisfaction in your work.

The value of operating with integrity in sales is immeasurable. By embracing this timeless virtue, you'll not only close more deals and build a rock-solid reputation but also set the stage for sustained high performance and a lasting legacy of success. So, make integrity the cornerstone of your sales career - and watch as your performance soars to new heights.

COMMANDMENT 8:
THOU SHALT STRIKE WHEN THE IRON IS HOT

Develop a keen sense for recognizing buying signals and employ the most fitting closing technique at the opportune moment.

Being able to identify and interpret buying signals is a well-developed sixth sense, catapulting you into the league of sales superheroes, while the amateurs are still trying to figure out which end of the phone to talk into. The ability to sense when a prospect is ready to buy and to transition smoothly from selling to closing is the level-up cheat code that turns good salespeople into cape-wearing closers.

So, how do you develop this invaluable skill? It all starts with understanding that buying signals can come in various shapes and forms. They can be as subtle as a flicker of interest in a prospect's eyes or as overt as an outright request for pricing information. Your mission, should you choose to accept it, is to become a master of detecting these signals and honing your instincts so you can sense when a prospect is ripe for the close.

Some common buying signals you should keep an eye out for include:

- Asking about pricing, payment options, or financing.

- Inquiring about product availability, delivery timelines, or implementation processes.

- Requesting additional information, a product demonstration, or a follow-up meeting.

- Repeating or rephrasing their needs, pain points, or desired outcomes.

- Exhibiting positive body language, such as leaning in, nodding, maintaining eye contact, or even mirroring your gestures.

Now, once you've become adept at recognizing these buying signals, the real magic happens when you learn to stop talking and shift gears into closing mode. I cannot stress this enough: when you sense that a prospect is ready to sign on the dotted line, it's time to zip your lips and let the close unfold.

Why is this so important? Well, as any seasoned sales pro will tell you, continuing to sell when a prospect is ready to buy can actually hurt your chances of closing the deal. You wouldn't add bait to a hook that's already caught a fish - it's unnecessary and, quite frankly, counterproductive.

So, how do you make that seamless transition from selling to closing when you detect those precious buying signals? Here are a few tips to help you master the art of transitioning to the close:

PAUSE AND TAKE A BREATH

Give yourself a moment to process the buying signal and mentally prepare for the next phase. This pause can also create a sense of anticipation in the prospect, making them more receptive to your closing moves.

SUMMARIZE THE VALUE YOU'RE OFFERING

Before moving to the close, quickly recap the key benefits of your product or service and how they address the prospect's needs. This serves as a powerful reminder of why they're ready to buy in the first place. Pro tip: It's best to use this if you've gone off topic and need to circle back before the close question.

ASK A CLOSING QUESTION

Guide the prospect toward a commitment by asking a carefully crafted closing question. For example, "Is there any reason you would like to stick with *<insert their current solution or problem they're facing>*?"

LISTEN AND RESPOND ACCORDINGLY

Once you've asked your closing question, give the prospect space to respond, and pay close attention to their answer. If they voice any lingering concerns or objections, address them head-on before attempting to close again.

SEAL IT WITH ASSUMPTIVE CONFIDENCE

When you sense that the prospect is ready to commit, wrap up the close with a confident and decisive statement and a call to action, such as, *"From here, it's just a matter of getting you approved. Do you have your ID?"* Remember, confidence is contagious - when you exude certainty, your prospect is more likely to feel confident in their decision as well.

KEEP IT SIMPLE AND STRAIGHTFORWARD

Honor Commandment 2. Don't overcomplicate the closing process with unnecessary jargon or complex explanations. Your goal is to make it as easy and painless as possible for the prospect to accept moving forward.

BE MINDFUL OF BODY LANGUAGE

As you transition to the close, maintain strong eye contact, use open and relaxed gestures, and lean in slightly to convey your genuine interest and commitment to the prospect's success. This non-verbal communication can speak volumes and help solidify the deal.

Developing a keen sense for recognizing buying signals and knowing when to stop talking and move to the next step of closing are essential skills for any sales professional looking to rise above the competition. The ability to smoothly transition from selling to closing not only increases your chances of sealing the deal but also elevates your status as a true sales powerhouse.

It's time to sharpen your senses, fine-tune your instincts, and master the art of striking when opportunity calls. And remember, when the iron is hot and the opportunity presents itself, don't hesitate - strike with confidence and finesse, seizing the moment to secure the deal.

COMMANDMENT 9:
THOU SHALT EMBRACE THE C.E.C. MINDSET
(CLOSE EVERY CUSTOMER)

Adopt an attitude of confidence, positivity, and unwavering determination to succeed in every sales situation with integrity.

When it comes to closing a sale, there's one rule that should be etched into your very soul: leave no stone unturned.

Great closers are great salespeople, but great salespeople aren't always great closers. You need a unique blend of tenacity, finesse, and strategic thinking to push that sale across the finish line. But if you can harness that power, you'll be a force to be reckoned with.

If you want to be a top performer in sales, you've got to adopt a mindset of closing every customer whom you interact with. Now, I know what you're thinking - that's impossible. But hear me out.

The truth is, you're not going to close every customer. It's just not going to happen. But here's the thing - the C.E.C. mindset is invaluable to becoming a disruptive top performer. It's the mentality that separates the average from the exceptional. Just one or two extra sales a week that you otherwise thought were impossible can easily double your sales results for the month.

So, how do you adopt this mindset?

EMBRACE THE "ALL OR NOTHING" ATTITUDE

You've gotta be an all-or-nothing person in the sales world. No half-hearted attempts, no giving up when the going gets tough. You need to believe, with every fiber of your being, that you can and WILL close every customer you interact with. This isn't about being cocky or overconfident - it's about having the resilience and commitment to fight for every sale like it's your last. When you have this unyielding mindset, you'll become an unstoppable force.

GET SUCCESS AMNESIA

Perhaps the most valuable piece of advice in this book is this idea here. Elite sales professionals recognize the value of resetting their mindset for every potential customer they engage. They leave past accomplishments behind and approach each new opportunity with a fresh perspective, as though they were under immense financial pressure. This relentless determination to succeed in each interaction propels them to consistently deliver gold-star sticker-worthy results, elevating them to the status of disruptive sales leaders in their field.

I'm serious. If you don't retain anything else, retain this: I don't care if you just raked in $10k from the previous appointment two hours ago, you better go into the next appointment as if you're three months behind in rent and the baby is out of milk. This single mental game of success amnesia will single-handedly alter your DNA, reconstructing its strands with fortified tenacity and hunger for disruption.

UNLEASH YOUR INNER PIT BULL

A top performer never backs down from a challenge, and neither should you. A pit bull doesn't let go of its target once its jaws are locked. You must be relentless in your own pursuit. When faced with objections or setbacks, don't just roll over and accept defeat. Sink your teeth in, stay persistent, and tackle those obstacles head-on. Find creative solutions, offer alternatives, and do whatever it takes to win the customer over while maintaining integrity and a well-balanced approach that avoids inflaming the customer. Persistence, my friend, is the name of the game.

CONTINUOUSLY REFINE YOUR SKILLS

To adopt the C.E.C. mindset you need to be willing to put in the work. Constantly refine your skills by seeking out new training, attending workshops, and learning from the best in the business. Study your own sales calls and meetings, analyze your successes and failures, and always look for ways to improve. Remember, there's no such thing as perfection - only progress.

STAY HUNGRY, STAY FOOLISH

The moment you think you've "made it" is the moment you start to stagnate. A true top performer never stops learning, growing, and pushing their limits. Embrace the mindset of always striving for more, even when you're at the top of your game. Stay hungry, stay foolish, and never settle for mediocrity.

Ultimately, you must have a fierce commitment to exhaust every option to close. You've got to be willing to leave no stone unturned and explore every angle and resource to make it happen. That means asking the right questions, offering incentives, leveraging your network, and getting creative. It means following up, even when it feels like you're getting nowhere. It means being persistent, but strategic in your approach.

It's not just the tactics - it's the attitude. You've got to approach every customer interaction with the mindset of closing. That means being confident, assertive, and committed. It means believing in yourself and your product or service. It means being passionate about what you do and why you do it.

The more you adopt this mindset, the more you'll see results. You'll start to close more customers, build stronger relationships, and exceed the performance levels of the average and even the best.

COMMANDMENT 10:
THOU SHALT NEVER REST ON THY LAURELS

Continually invest in thy personal and professional growth affairs, refining thy talents and remaining open to new strategies, insights, and opportunities.

You've just closed a massive deal, landed that mega client, or obliterated your sales target. Time to kick back, relax, and bask in the afterglow of your achievements, right? Negative, bucko. Riding the dopamine wave and resting on your laurels is about as smart as using an umbrella in a hurricane. Complacency is the Achilles' heel of your Herculean sales ascension.

THE SALES GAME IS A CHAMELEON ON ACID

The world of sales is like a chameleon on acid – an ever-evolving beast, my friends. Constantly shifting colors and adapting to its environment at breakneck speed. If you rest on your laurels, you'll quickly find yourself left behind. Stay ahead of the curve by keeping your finger on the pulse of industry trends, embracing new technologies, and learning from the trailblazers who are redefining the game.

IT'S YOU VS YOU: PUSH THE ENVELOPE

Sustainable results lie in competing with the most formidable opponent of all - yourself. When you're selling at high levels, it's all too easy to get caught up in the rat race of comparing yourself to your peers. A key component to true sales mastery lies not in outperforming others, but in outperforming your own past achievements. By focusing on your own growth and development, you'll not only avoid the soul-sucking trap of envy but also unlock your true potential. Set ambitious goals, challenge your limits, and explore new strategies and techniques to take your sales game to stratospheric heights. In doing so, you'll not only surpass your own expectations but naturally leave your competition eating dust.

COMPLACENCY IS A SLIPPERY SLOPE

When you're at the top of your game, it's all too easy to slip into a false sense of security, thinking you've got it all figured out. But let me tell you, you might as well be a banana peel on ice. Before you know it, you'll be sliding down the slippery slope of mediocrity, wondering where it all went wrong. Don't let complacency be your downfall. Stay humble, stay hungry, and never stop learning.

THE PURSUIT OF EXCELLENCE IS A MARATHON, NOT A SPRINT

Achieving greatness is a lifelong pursuit, not a one-time deal. It's a marathon, not a sprint. It takes time, dedication, and relentless effort to reach the upper echelons of sales royalty. So, don't treat your victories as an excuse to rest on your laurels. Instead, use them as fuel to propel you towards even greater heights.

The moment you decide to rest on your laurels is the moment you sign your own career death warrant. It's a dangerous game of Russian roulette that no high-level closer should ever play. Remember, success is a fickle mistress, and she'll drop you fast if you take her for granted.

10 COMMANDMENTS CONCLUSION

Stay nimble, stay driven, and never underestimate the power of reinvention. Keep your skills polished and your mindset razor-focused, because, in the pursuit of disruptive levels of success, there's no room for complacency.

Always be on the lookout for opportunities to learn and grow, even when you're basking in the warm glow of your hard-earned achievements. After all, the true measure of a sales superstar isn't their ability to close deals - it's their unwavering commitment to excellence, no matter the circumstances.

Keep pushing forward, and never stop chasing that elusive sales dragon. Because, as any seasoned closer will tell you, the thrill of the chase is half the fun. And who knows? With the right attitude, a healthy dose of grit, and a penchant for witty analogies (if I do say so myself), you might just find yourself joining the ranks of the sales elite - with no laurels in sight.

Remember, the world is your oyster, and the only thing standing between you and greatness is a little thing called complacency. So, do yourself a favor: kick that smug sense of satisfaction to the curb, and keep reaching for the stars. After all, as they say, the sky's the limit - and you're more than capable of soaring to unimaginable heights.

10 Closer Commandments

1. Thou Shalt Set Proper Expectations

2. Thou Shalt Cut The Fluff

3. Thou Shalt Master The Art Of Listening

4. Thou Shalt Ask Great Questions

5. Thou Shalt Be A Storytelling Wizard

6. Thou Shalt Honor Structure

7. Thou Shalt Operate With Unwavering Integrity

8. Thou Shalt Strike When The Iron Is Hot

9. Thou Shalt Embrace The C.E.C. Mindset

10. Thou Shalt Never Rest On Thy Laurels

CHAPTER 9

ELEVATION IN OBSERVATION

When I first started out in sales, I had no idea what to expect. I guess I was expecting to show up on my first day with my trainer and go through this intense training that would give me everything I needed to master selling. While that turned out to be true to some degree, it wasn't in the form of one-on-one direct training. My direct training was no more than a 10-question quiz typed up on a Word document and a quick run-through of how to process a sale in the portal we used.

"This is going to be fun", I thought.

On my second day, it was filled with basketball-related YouTube videos, listening in on his personal calls, and watching his casual flirty banter with all the ladies in surrounding stores. Not that anything was wrong with that, he was able to balance that and still get by comfortably. While it seemed like a laid-back work environment most could enjoy, I understood that I didn't have the security he had. He was a top producer in the company that also happened to be great friends with the owner.

If I would have adopted those habits, I knew I'd be gone, fast. So, instead of expecting this transformative sales training, I used what I could to train myself. After all, he was one of the most charismatic salespeople I had seen.

From that moment forward, I documented every customer interaction – the words he used, his jokes, body language, outreach practices to the bypassing customer, how he asked for the sale, etc. I wanted to dissect every detail that was contributing to his success.

By week two, after studying pages of notes, I had his whole style down to a tee. I cherry-picked what I loved, discarded what I didn't, and added my own personality to make it authentic.

Looking back, I was lucky to have had such a "meh" direct training experience. It bred a high level of resourcefulness and creativity that brought out an elevated version of myself. And developing that skill so early on served me well from that moment forward.

When I first started to observe and take notes to adopt what he was doing well, I didn't really look at it as a strategy. My thought process hadn't quite developed into intentional growth-oriented strategies, as if I was carrying out something you'd pick up from a self-help book. In fact, I probably hadn't read a single self-help book in my life at the time. It was more of an instinctive action I took out of necessity to survive.

Once it finally clicked that it could be, in fact, a purposefully carried out strategy, I started to analyze other areas where I could execute the same practice of observing others to elevate other skills. This led to picking up skills from experts across every layer of business, from finance and HR to operations, sales, and marketing.

If you want to achieve greatness, you just need to study greatness. That means observing and learning from top performers across any industry. Whether you're a new salesperson looking to improve your skills or an experienced business owner seeking to take your business from $1m to $10m, studying top performers can give you the knowledge, inspiration, and motivation you need to succeed.

So why is observing top performers so important? For starters, it allows you to learn from experience. Top performers have been through countless situations and have developed strategies and techniques that work. By observing and studying their behavior, you can gain insight into how they approach certain situations, learn from their successes and failures, and apply these lessons to your own approach.

But it's not just about learning from experience. Studying top performers also helps you understand best practices. These are the techniques, habits, and processes that top performers use to achieve success. By observing these best practices and incorporating them into your own approach, you can improve your skills and rapidly increase your levels of success. Ultimately, this allows you to take years of experience and condense it into just a few months, weeks, or even days of learning and implementing.

This habit also comes with an element of inspiration and motivation. Seeing top performers in action can be incredibly inspiring and motivating. It shows you what is possible and encourages you to push yourself to achieve more. It can also help you stay focused on your goals and keep you motivated during difficult times.

Observing top performers is like looking through a prism to unlock the secrets of success. Just as a prism refracts light into its individual colors, observing top performers allows you to break down their skills and techniques into their individual components. By analyzing and understanding these components, you can then apply them in your own unique way to achieve success in your field. It's not about copying what others have done, but rather taking what you've learned and using it to create something truly innovative and exceptional. In the same way that a prism can create a beautiful rainbow of colors, observing top performers can help you create something truly amazing and extraordinary.

INNOVATION IN OBSERVATION

Throughout history, businesses have used these same techniques in a way to gain insight and knowledge that have helped them achieve their goals. By borrowing from others' innovations and approaches, companies have continued to improve their own businesses and stay ahead of the competition. The most successful companies are those that are willing to learn from others and adapt to changing market conditions. For example:

1. APPLE AND XEROX —

In the early 1980s, Apple founder Steve Jobs was given a tour of Xerox's Palo Alto Research Center. During the tour, Jobs saw a demo of the Xerox Alto, a computer with a graphical user interface and mouse that allowed users to interact with the computer using a pointing device. Jobs recognized the potential of this technology and immediately began working on his own version, which eventually became the Macintosh. By borrowing from Xerox's innovations, Apple was able to create a revolutionary product that changed the course of computing history.[1]

2. GOOGLE AND AMAZON —

Google and Amazon are two of the most successful companies in the world, but they achieved their success in very different ways. Google became the dominant search engine by providing the most relevant search results, while Amazon built its business on providing the best customer experience. However, both companies learned from each other to improve their own businesses. Google studied Amazon's customer-centric approach to improve its own search algorithms, while Amazon learned from Google's data-driven approach to marketing and advertising to improve its own business.[2]

3. NETFLIX AND BLOCKBUSTER —

Blockbuster was once the dominant player in the video rental market, but it failed to adapt to changing technologies and consumer habits. Netflix, on the other hand, recognized the potential of streaming video and invested heavily in the technology. By learning from Blockbuster's mistakes and embracing new technologies, Netflix was able to become the dominant player in the market and transform the way people consume media.[3]

4. TESLA AND FORD —

While Tesla may be the new kid on the block when it comes to electric cars, they certainly didn't reinvent the wheel. In fact, Tesla's founder, Elon Musk, has openly stated that he learned a lot from Henry Ford and his innovative approach to manufacturing. Ford was the first to introduce the assembly line, which revolutionized the way cars were produced. Tesla has taken this a step further by utilizing robots and automation to create a more efficient and cost-effective manufacturing process.[4]

5. ZARA AND TOYOTA —

Zara is one of the most successful fashion retailers in the world, and they owe a lot of their success to Toyota. Zara's founder, Amancio Ortega, learned a lot from Toyota's lean manufacturing techniques, which are designed to minimize waste and increase efficiency. By applying these techniques to the fashion industry, Zara was able to create a fast and flexible supply chain that allows them to quickly respond to changing trends and customer demands.[5]

The truth is, no one person or business has all the answers. That's why it's important to learn from others and take inspiration from their successes. Whether it's looking to Uber for user rating systems, Apple for mobile technology, Virgin for company culture, or Trello for collaboration tools, there is always something to be learned from those who have disrupted their industry.

THE FAAR FRAMEWORK

To achieve disruptive levels of sales, it is essential to adopt a systematic approach that encourages growth and development. One such framework is what I call the F.A.A.R. framework, which stands for Find, Analyze, Adopt, and Refine. This comprehensive method is designed to help salespeople build on their strengths, identify and learn from successful role models, and consistently refine their skills to maintain a competitive edge.

FIND: IDENTIFYING ROLE MODELS FOR SUCCESS

The first step in the F.A.A.R. framework is to identify successful individuals who possess the skills or traits you wish to acquire. These role models may come from various industries, backgrounds, or even your personal network. The idea is to learn from those who excel in areas such as communication, charisma, or humor, and emulate their strengths to enhance your sales abilities.

Think of it as assembling a dream team of mentors. As the saying goes, "You are the average of the five people you spend the most time with." By surrounding yourself with successful individuals, you can absorb their winning habits and thought patterns.

ANALYZE: THE DEEP DIVE INTO SKILLS AND TRAITS

Once you have identified your role models, the next step is to immerse yourself in the information related to their skills or traits. This involves a deep dive into their work, analyzing every detail to understand the secrets behind their success. Study their articles, books, speeches, or interviews, and pay close attention to the techniques they employ.

For example, if you wish to improve your public speaking abilities, closely observe the way some of the most viewed TED talk speakers engage with their audience, how they structure their content, and their use of body language. By analyzing these details, you can identify the critical components that contribute to their success and incorporate them into your own sales approach.

ADOPT: PUTTING ANALYSIS INTO PRACTICE

The next phase in the F.A.A.R. framework is to adopt the knowledge, skills, and insights gained from your role models. This step is crucial because learning from others only adds value when you put the lessons into practice. As you adopt these newfound techniques, trust your instincts to guide you on what to embrace or discard.

Consider this phase as customizing your sales toolkit. You don't need to be a carbon copy of your role models. Instead, adapt their techniques to fit your unique personality and strengths. By doing so, you create a more authentic and elite version of yourself that resonates with your target audience.

REFINE: THE PURSUIT OF PROGRESSION

The final component of the F.A.A.R. framework is refinement. It's essential to recognize that even the most successful salespeople never reach a state of perfection; they simply focus on continuous progression. This commitment to constant improvement helps them stay ahead of the competition and maintain their status as elite performers.

To refine your skills, embrace a growth mindset, and be willing to adapt to new information and trends in your industry. Set aside time for regular reflection and self-assessment, identifying areas where you can improve or learn from recent experiences. Continuously sharpen your skills and knowledge to ensure you're always at the top of your game.

CONCLUSION

The F.A.A.R. framework provides a comprehensive roadmap for achieving disruptive levels of sales success. By identifying successful role models, analyzing their techniques, adopting their strengths, and refining your skills, you can consistently outperform your peers and maintain a competitive edge in the sales arena. Embrace this systematic approach to growth and development, and you'll soon find yourself on the path to sales disruption.

Think of the F.A.A.R. framework as a map that guides you through uncharted territory, helping you navigate the constantly evolving landscape of the sales world. By following this map, you'll be better equipped to face the challenges and obstacles that may arise along the way. As you continue to grow and adapt, you'll also discover new opportunities and strategies that can propel you further toward your goals.

That's why it's so critical to continue to learn and refine what you've adopted. The most elite never reaches a level of perfection, they just focus on progression. There's always another level to hit. Another enhancement to be made. More information to absorb. This requires even the best to be obsessed with continued learning and growth.

Imagine if Kobe, LeBron, Steph, MJ, or your favorite star player stopped training at the height of their success. Their success was and is a result of them continually pushing themselves to improve, striving to break their personal records, and achieving new milestones. The same principle applies to sales professionals. By adhering to the F.A.A.R. framework, you commit yourself to the ongoing process of self-improvement, ensuring that you're always at the forefront of your field.

As you progress through the F.A.A.R. framework, you'll develop a keen understanding of what works for you and what doesn't. This self-awareness will enable you to optimize your sales approach, fine-tuning it to match your unique strengths and circumstances. The result is a sales strategy that is both efficient and effective, allowing you to consistently outperform your competition.

Moreover, the F.A.A.R. framework fosters a sense of resilience and adaptability, two qualities that are invaluable in the ever-changing world of sales. As market conditions shift, customer preferences evolve, and new competitors emerge, you'll be well-equipped to adjust your approach accordingly. This agility will help you stay ahead of the curve and maintain your status as a top-performing sales professional.

In essence, the F.A.A.R. framework is more than just a set of steps - it's a mindset that encourages growth, innovation, and excellence. By embracing this mindset and applying the principles of Find, Analyze, Adopt, and Refine, you'll be well on your way to achieving disruptive levels of sales success.

So, as you implement this framework, remember to keep your eyes on the horizon and your mind open to new possibilities. With the F.A.A.R. framework as your guide, you'll be well-equipped to navigate the ever-changing landscape of the sales world, overcome the challenges that may arise, and ultimately, achieve the kind of success that truly sets you apart from the rest.

CHAPTER 10

THE CLOSER'S ASCENSION

Embarking on the path to becoming a disruptive sales leader is a journey filled with growth, challenges, and continuous learning. Along the way, sales professionals will encounter different stages of development, each with its own unique set of skills, characteristics, and opportunities for growth. To provide a clear roadmap for this journey, I present the Five Levels of Closers, a comprehensive guide that illustrates the progression from Novice Closer to Disruptive Sales Leader.

The Five Levels of Closers is an essential structure for understanding and navigating the complex landscape of sales closing mastery. By recognizing the skills and abilities inherent to each level, sales professionals can focus their efforts on the development and improvement of the specific competencies needed to advance to the next stage. Each level builds upon the last, culminating in the ultimate achievement of becoming 5th level status.

This journey, while challenging, is far from impossible. All it takes is some classic grit, a laser-sharp focus, and a growth mindset that would put a Chia Pet to shame. With this level of commitment, you can steadily progress through each level, ultimately reaching the pinnacle of sales closing mastery. The Five Levels of Closers serves as both a roadmap and an invitation to embark on this journey, providing a clear and concise guide for those who are ready to take the first step toward achieving the highest level.

As you venture through these levels, remember that the journey is as important as the destination. Embrace the challenges, toast to the milestones, and above all, never stop learning. With the Five Levels of Closers as your guide, you will be well-equipped to rise through the ranks and achieve the ultimate goal of becoming a Disruptive Sales Leader.

LEVEL 1: THE NOVICE CLOSER

The Novice Closer is an eager newcomer to the sales world, brimming with potential but lacking the experience and refined skill set of more seasoned professionals. With dedication and guidance, the Novice Closer can develop into a formidable force in the sales arena.

CURRENT SKILLS

Basic understanding of the sales process, active listening, and the ability to ask relevant questions.

SKILLS TO DEVELOP

Advanced questioning techniques, rapport building, handling objections, and mastering closing techniques.

BEST PRACTICES FOR GROWTH

The Novice Closer should seek out mentorship, invest in professional development resources, and practice sales presentations regularly to hone their skills.

LEVEL 2: THE PERSUADER

The Persuader has gained some experience and developed a more sophisticated understanding of the sales process. They're capable of closing deals but may struggle with more challenging prospects or complex sales scenarios.

CURRENT SKILLS

Solid understanding of the sales process, rapport building, some experience handling objections, and familiarity with closing techniques.

SKILLS TO DEVELOP

Confidence in addressing complex sales scenarios, advanced objection handling, and the ability to adapt to different buyer personalities.

BEST PRACTICES FOR GROWTH

The Persuader should seek out new challenges, shadow top-performing colleagues, and continue investing in skill development through training and workshops.

LEVEL 3: THE DYNAMO

The Dynamo is a skilled closer, adept at navigating various sales situations and consistently sealing the deal. They have a strong track record of success but may still have room for growth in becoming a true sales titan.

CURRENT SKILLS

Expertise in the sales process, strong rapport building, advanced objection handling, and mastery of various closing techniques.

SKILLS TO DEVELOP

Creating a personal sales style, understanding buyer psychology, and leveraging storytelling for persuasive impact.

BEST PRACTICES FOR GROWTH

The Dynamo should refine their personal sales style, study the art of persuasion and storytelling, and seek feedback from colleagues to identify areas for improvement.

LEVEL 4: THE SALES ALCHEMIST

The Sales Alchemist has mastered the art of turning ash into gold. They're a masterful closer, capable of turning even the most challenging prospects into loyal customers. They possess a deep understanding of buyer psychology and excel at crafting compelling narratives to drive sales success.

CURRENT SKILLS

Personal sales style, expertise in buyer psychology, persuasive storytelling, and an exceptional closing record.

SKILLS TO DEVELOP

Building a personal brand, refining emotional intelligence, and developing the ability to spot new opportunities.

BEST PRACTICES FOR GROWTH

The Sales Alchemist should focus on developing their personal brand, building a network of industry contacts, and keeping a pulse on market trends to identify untapped opportunities.

LEVEL 5: THE DISRUPTIVE SALES LEADER

The Disruptive Sales Leader is the ultimate closer, setting the benchmark for pure disruptive excellence. They possess an uncanny ability to shatter expectations, redefine industry norms, and consistently achieve unprecedented sales results.

CURRENT SKILLS

Personal brand mastery, emotional intelligence, spotting opportunities, and an unparalleled closing record.

SKILLS TO DEVELOP

Strategic vision, leadership, and a relentless drive for innovation.

BEST PRACTICES FOR GROWTH

The DSL should seek out leadership roles, mentor aspiring sales professionals, and always strive to stay ahead of the curve through continuous learning and innovation.

Embarking on the journey from Novice Closer to DSL is much like scaling a mountain - each level demands increasing effort, perseverance, and determination. But with the right mindset and commitment to growth, you'll find yourself standing at the summit, surveying the landscape of sales mastery from the highest peak.

As you ascend through the ranks of closers, remember to celebrate your victories, learn from your setbacks, and continually strive for improvement. The path to sales greatness may be strenuous, but the rewards are well worth the effort.

Keep in mind that there is no one-size-fits-all approach to mastering the art of closing. Each individual must tailor their path to suit their unique strengths, weaknesses, and personal style. The key to success is finding the right balance between tried-and-true best practices and innovative strategies that set you apart from the competition.

Also, never forget the importance of staying humble and maintaining a learner's mindset, even as you reach the apex of sales prowess. In the words of the timeless Socrates, "The only true wisdom is in knowing you know nothing."[1] Or like I say, "the knowledge of your own ignorance is a quick sprint to the shelf to grab this book." Either way, embrace a philosophy of constant growth, and you'll find that the speed of your journey to joining the 5th level of the most elite class of closers moves at the same rate as the learning velocity.

By diligently working through each level, honing the necessary skills, and embracing a growth mindset, you'll find yourself well on your way to becoming an unstoppable force. So, put on your metaphorical climbing gear and start your ascent today - the view from the top is simply unbeatable.

As you continue to embark on your quest to become a disruptive sales leader, it's essential to recognize that the journey doesn't end at the summit. The world of sales is ever-evolving, with new techniques, technologies, and challenges emerging constantly. To maintain your status as a top closer, you must remain vigilant, staying up to date with the latest trends and adapting to the ever-changing sales landscape.

One way to ensure you stay at the forefront of the sales world is by surrounding yourself with like-minded individuals who share your passion for growth and success. Engage in professional networks, attend conferences, and join online forums dedicated to sales excellence. By immersing yourself in a community of ambitious sales professionals, you'll find a wealth of resources and inspiration to fuel your continued ascent.

Another crucial aspect of maintaining your edge as a closer is investing in self-care and personal development. Sales can be a demanding and high-pressure field, and it's vital to prioritize your well-being to perform at your best. Develop a routine that promotes physical and mental health, whether that involves exercise, meditation, or spending time with loved ones. Remember, even the most formidable sales professionals need to recharge and rejuvenate to maintain their momentum.

Lastly, always be on the lookout for opportunities to mentor and support those who are following in your footsteps. By sharing your knowledge, experience, and insights with up-and-coming sales professionals, you not only help them achieve their goals but also reinforce your own expertise and strengthen your understanding of sales fundamentals.

In conclusion, the journey to becoming a disruptive sales leader is a continuous and dynamic process, requiring dedication, adaptability, and resilience. Embrace the challenges, celebrate your achievements, and never stop striving for greatness. The path may be steep and the road may be long, but when you channel your inner mountain goat, you'll climb the most treacherous verticals like a caffeinated squirrel.

THE 5 LEVELS OF CLOSERS

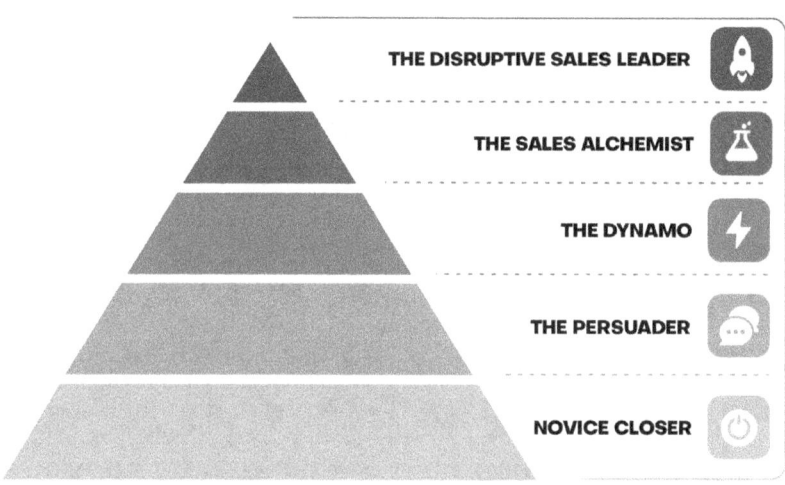

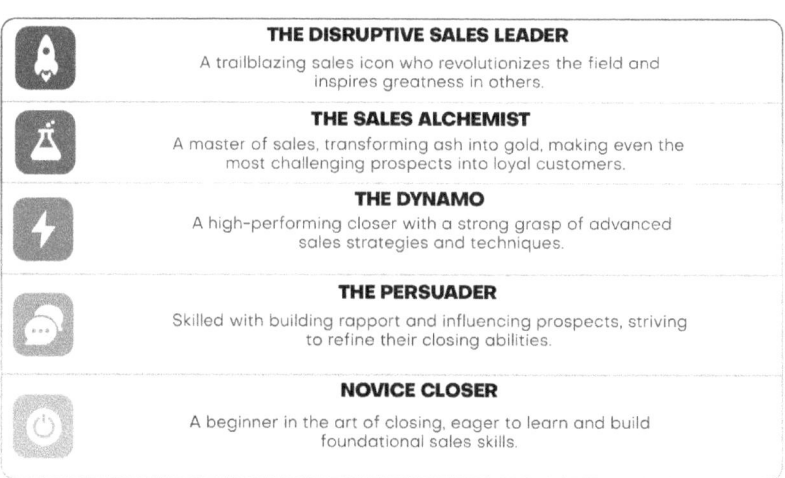

THE DISRUPTIVE SALES LEADER
A trailblazing sales icon who revolutionizes the field and inspires greatness in others.

THE SALES ALCHEMIST
A master of sales, transforming ash into gold, making even the most challenging prospects into loyal customers.

THE DYNAMO
A high-performing closer with a strong grasp of advanced sales strategies and techniques.

THE PERSUADER
Skilled with building rapport and influencing prospects, striving to refine their closing abilities.

NOVICE CLOSER
A beginner in the art of closing, eager to learn and build foundational sales skills.

THE ASCENSION FRAMEWORK: A GUIDED PATH TO DISRUPTIVE SALES LEADERSHIP

While the journey to Disruptive Sales Leadership is undeniably challenging, having a structured, step-by-step framework to follow can make all the difference. The Ascension Framework is designed to provide the guidance and support you need as you work through each stage of the Closer's Ascension. By adhering to this framework, you'll be well-equipped to tackle the obstacles and opportunities that come your way, transforming you into an unstoppable sales leader in the process.

ASSESS AND REFLECT

Begin your ascension by taking stock of your current skills, strengths, and weaknesses. This process of self-assessment will provide you with a clear understanding of your starting point and the areas you need to focus on as you progress through the levels. Don't be afraid to solicit feedback from colleagues, mentors, or managers to gain an even more accurate picture of your current abilities.

SET CLEAR GOALS AND DEADLINES

With a solid understanding of your current skillset, set specific, measurable, achievable, relevant, and time-bound (SMART) goals for your development. Establish clear deadlines for when you aim to reach each new level of the ascension and break down these long-term goals into smaller milestones to make the journey more manageable.

ADOPT BEST PRACTICES

As you work to develop the skills and abilities necessary for each level, embrace the best practices and proven strategies that have propelled other sales professionals to success. While it's essential to tailor your approach to your unique style and strengths, incorporating these tried-and-true methods will help you build a strong foundation for your growth.

INNOVATE AND EXPERIMENT

While adopting best practices is crucial, it's equally important to think outside the box and explore new techniques and tactics that will set you apart from the competition. Embrace your creativity and be willing to take risks as you search for innovative ways to elevate your sales performance.

EVALUATE AND ADJUST

Regularly assess your progress toward your goals and be prepared to make adjustments as needed. This may involve revisiting your goals, refining your strategies, or seeking additional support from mentors or coaches. Remember, the path to disruptive sales leadership is rarely a straight line, and adaptability is key to success.

EMBODY THE TRIPLE C PATH TO VICTORY

As you continue to ascend the ranks of the Closer's Ascension, don't forget to integrate the principles of the Care Champ and the Creator roles into your approach. By harmonizing these three critical components, you'll unlock the true potential of the Disruptive Sales Leader.

PAY IT FORWARD

As you achieve your goals and reach new heights in your sales career, look for opportunities to mentor and support those who are just beginning their own journeys. Sharing your knowledge and experience will not only benefit others but also reinforce your own expertise and understanding of sales excellence.

In conclusion, the Ascension Framework is designed to provide the structure and support you need as you embark on the challenging yet rewarding journey to becoming a Disruptive Sales Leader. By following this roadmap and maintaining a growth mindset, you'll be well-prepared to tackle the obstacles that come your way and ultimately achieve unprecedented levels of sales success. So, set your sights high, and let the Ascension Framework guide you to greatness.

THE CLOSER'S LEGACY

As you ascend the levels of the Closer's Ascension and find success as a closer, it's essential to recognize the broader impact your achievements can have on those around you. By harnessing your skills, expertise, and experiences to inspire others, mentor the next generation of closers, and give back to your community, you can leave a lasting legacy that transcends your individual accomplishments.

INSPIRING OTHERS TO EXCEL

Your journey to the top of the Closer's Ascension is a testament to what is possible with dedication, resilience, and a commitment to growth. By sharing your story, celebrating your victories, and embracing vulnerability when discussing your challenges, you can inspire others to strive for greatness and pursue their own paths to success. Embodying the principles of the Triple C Path to Victory and living these values every day will serve as a powerful example for others to follow.

MENTORING THE NEXT GENERATION OF CLOSERS

As a disruptive sales leader, you have a wealth of knowledge and experience to share with those who are just beginning their own journeys. By mentoring up-and-coming sales professionals, you can help them navigate the challenges and obstacles they face, empowering them to achieve their full potential. Additionally, mentoring offers a unique opportunity to reflect on your own growth and development, solidifying your expertise and deepening your understanding of the sales process.

GIVING BACK TO YOUR COMMUNITY

Success in sales is not only about personal achievement but also about using your skills and resources to create a positive impact on the world around you. Consider giving back to your community by volunteering your time, donating a portion of your earnings, or supporting local initiatives that align with your values. By leveraging your success to create meaningful change, you can contribute to a lasting legacy that extends far beyond your individual accomplishments.

LEAVING A LASTING IMPACT

To create a truly enduring legacy, it's essential to think about the long-term impact of your actions and the example you set for others. Cultivate a reputation for integrity, professionalism, and genuine care for your customers, colleagues, and community. Embrace the principles of the Care Champ, the Creator, and the Closer in every aspect of your life, and strive to be a force for good in all that you do.

In conclusion, the journey to becoming a disruptive sales leader is about more than just personal success; it's about using your abilities and experiences to inspire others, mentor the next generation, and leave a lasting impact on the world. By embracing the principles of the Closer's Legacy, you can ensure that your achievements resonate far beyond your sales career, creating a ripple effect that will inspire countless others to pursue their own paths to greatness. As the famous Chinese philosopher Lao Tzu once said, "*A journey of a thousand miles begins with a single step.*"[1] So, take that first step today, and let your legacy as a disruptive sales leader begin to unfold.

CHAPTER 11

FIND, YOUR CUSTOMER

For many salespeople, closing can be both exciting and nerve-racking, as it requires high levels of confidence, disciplined persistence, a flare of finesse, a deep understanding of your customer's needs and motivations, and the mental fortitude to stomach the ups and downs that come with.

Throughout my career, I'm dealt with customers of all ages and ethnicities with a wide range of professional backgrounds,   income levels, and buying wants and needs. These interactions have allowed me to understand the different customer types, their characteristics, and how to identify them. And more importantly, how to segment those customers allowed me to tailor my marketing and sales strategies to each customer group to close in the most efficient and effective way possible for maximum results.

In this chapter, we'll delve into just that. We'll explore the key strategies, tactics, tips, and actionable insights that you can apply to any closing scenario. From understanding the psychology of persuasion to mastering the art of objection handling, I'll cover all the essential skills and techniques that will take your closing game to the next level. But first, it starts with not only understanding yourself but the person across from you.

UNDERSTANDING YOUR CUSTOMER

It's no secret that customers are the lifeblood of your business. If you've been in sales, you also understand that it's no secret that customers are not all created equal. Each customer has unique preferences, needs, and behaviors that affect how they interact with your business and what they expect from you. Understanding your customer type is the key to navigating through the sales journey to close the deal.

F-I-N-D YOUR CUSTOMER

You'll find your customers to be segmented into one of four of these customer types. Understanding which category your customer falls into will unlock the door to a more personalized and relatable experience to earn their business.

F: "FACT FINDING FIONA"

Who Are They:

Analytical people are those who love data, facts, and logic. They're the type of people who will dig deep into the numbers to find the truth. They're methodical and precise, and they don't take anything at face value. They want to see proof, evidence, and hard facts before they make any decisions. These are the kind of people who won't make a move until they have all the information they need and could care less about the hype and any fluff you might try to incorporate into your pitch.

How to Win Them Over:

If you've dealt with an engineer or like-minded personality, you might already be convinced that analytical customers are impossible to please, but it really isn't true. These people are looking for a solution to their problem, just like any other customer. The key is to speak their language and show them that you understand their needs.

First, do your homework. Research your customer's industry, their company, and their specific needs. Find out what their pain points are and what they're looking for in a solution. Second, be prepared to provide them with solid evidence to support your claims. This could include case studies, customer testimonials, and data to show how your product or service has helped others in their industry.

Finally, and this is important, be patiently impatient. Analytical customers may take longer to make a decision than other customers, but it doesn't mean you can't close them on a first sit. They want to make sure they're making the right choice. If they feel they may need more information and reassurance, you'll want to extract that reservation and overcome it, which is talked about later in this chapter. So, be prepared to answer their questions, address their concerns, and provide them with the information they need to feel confident in their decision.

In short, winning over analytical customers requires a little extra effort and preparation, but it's well worth the chase. If you can provide them with solid evidence and speak their language, you can win them over and turn them into loyal customers. Because once they've made the decision, they have the highest stick rate, or not cancelling on you.

Summary:

- Provide detailed product specifications, case studies, or whitepapers that showcase the technical aspects of your offering.

- Be prepared to answer in-depth questions and back up your claims with solid evidence.

- Use charts, graphs, or other visuals to help convey complex information.

• Be patient and thorough, as this type of customer may require more time to make a decision.

Remember, to an analytical customer, knowledge is power. Equip them with the information they need to make an informed decision, and they're more likely to trust you and your product.

I: "I'LL TAKE IT ALL PAUL"

Who Are They:

The Pauls of the world know what they want and are easily influenced if you can deliver clearly that you have the solution. This customer type has a tendency to be impulsive and make decisions quickly, and is highly influenced by social proof, authority, and scarcity.

How to Win Them Over:

Appeal to their emotions, build rapport and use persuasive techniques such as storytelling, testimonials, and social proof. Once you've built confidence that you're the solution, shut up and move to the workstation. Seriously, don't talk yourself out of earning their business. This can be the easiest customer to gain, but I've witnessed salespeople feel that it was too easy, thinking that they need to continue to educate to earn their business. Over-talking can lead to more questions, or create concerns or reservations that didn't otherwise exist, which can lead the customer to want to do more research before they buy.

N: "NOT ENOUGH NATHAN"

Who Are They:

This guy is never satisfied until he feels he's got the most for his money and has the upper hand. These customers are assertive and competitive. They want to feel in control and may try to dominate the conversation or negotiation. They may challenge your authority or expertise and look for ways to gain an advantage.

How to Win Them Over:

Winning these customers over requires more psychological strategy. Here are two methods commonly used:

METHOD 1: ANCHORING

Anchoring is the perceived value of a product or service that's first introduced to the customer, a concept introduced by psychologists Daniel Kahneman and Amos Tversky.[1] That initial anchoring will set the tone for the entire negotiation and influences the buyer's perception of what is a fair price for the product or service. This bias essentially influences the way people evaluate subsequent information, skewing their judgments and perceptions. It's your traditional *"start high and land where you wanted them in the first place"*. While this tactic can be valuable, it's one I've rarely used. Unless used craftily, it can diminish the value of the product or service you're offering. This is why I use method 2, instead.

METHOD 2: VALUE AMPLIFICATION

As a sales professional, how can you stand your ground on price while still persuading your customer to buy? This is a strategy I like to call "Value Amplification." Customers don't buy on price, they buy on value. Haggling one single cent with a customer tells them that there's room for negotiation on price. Instead, stand firm, reinforce, and amplify your value. This amplification can be in the form of the value already covered or offering additional value that doesn't cost the company a dime.

Example:

"Nathan, there's nothing more I would like than to give this to you for free. The reality is, my company, myself, wouldn't be able to be here to serve you without sticking to these numbers. When you consider the value of x, y, and z, you're getting the best value, without question. The last thing that you want to do is wake up next week after you bought cheap, and end up with a feeling of regret because you're disappointed in the quality of service. How about this: let's get this in motion, and as an added value, I'll make sure you're account is assigned to the most loved, dedicated, and talented account manager we have here. Fair enough?"

D: "DANCE AROUND DONNA"

Despite any bad experiences you may have, this is an easy customer to close, but only if you are skilled enough to successfully extract any underlying objection and overcome it.

Who Are They:

These customers are indecisive and may avoid making a commitment or taking action. They may have fears, doubts, or uncertainties about the purchase and may need more time, reassurance, or guidance. To win over a "never make a decision that quick" customer, you need to understand their concerns, address their objections, and provide them with support, resources, and reinforced value. You should also offer them a clear and simple path to purchase, with options and incentives that make the decision easier.

How to Win Them Over:

Dancing with Donna can feel like you're two-stepping in a psychological minefield. One misstep and your prospects' reservations may dismantle the deal. However, with tact and strategic finesse, you can uncover their objections, address them directly, and successfully close the deal. This is referred to as the EVOC method in the next chapter.

CHAPTER 12

MASTERING THE CLOSE – THE E.V.O.C. METHOD

Closing a sale without a proper process can feel like trying to assemble a jigsaw puzzle in the dark. You know there's a beautiful picture waiting to be revealed, but without a clear strategy, you're left grasping at pieces and hoping for the best. That's where the undeniable importance of the E.V.O.C. Method comes into play, especially when you find yourself at the end of a sales presentation.

This method, standing tall as the "Extract, Validate, Overcome, and Close" superhero team of the sales world (minus the spandex), is the gravity-defying superpower that lifts the unnerving reservations, allowing you to overcome and close like the cape-wearing hero you are.

Without a methodical approach, you end up fumbling your way through the process, ultimately leaving both you and your prospect feeling like you're driving with a flat tire. This bumpy ride can result in lost sales, damaged customer relationships, and a bruised ego. Let's get into it.

E: EXTRACT CUSTOMER RESERVATIONS

Imagine you're a skilled archaeologist, and your mission is to unearth the precious artifacts hidden beneath the surface. In the world of sales, these artifacts are your customer's reservations. Your task is to extract them.

The key to discovering your customer's reservations is to ask open-ended questions that encourage them to articulate their thoughts and feelings. Instead of asking, "*Do you have any concerns?*", try this effective extraction method: *"Honest question for an honest answer – on a scale of 1 to 10, where do you find yourself? 10 being, 'let's get it in motion', 1 being, 'get out of my house!'"*.

Once they give you their number, say an 8, simply ask them, *"What's keeping you from being a 10? What are those two missing points?"*

If you hit a rock, and they just say they don't know or need to think about it, persist. Pose the question, *"If you had to put your finger on your biggest reservation, what would it be?"*

By framing the question in this way, you allow your customer to dig deeper into their concerns, ultimately providing you with valuable insights that can help you address their reservations. They're essentially handing you the key to unlock the time capsule you just discovered.

READ BETWEEN THE LINES

Occasionally, a customer's reservations are not explicitly expressed but are concealed within their body language or tone of voice. As an adept salesperson, it is your responsibility to read between the lines and identify these subtle cues. For instance, if a customer hesitates when discussing pricing, it might indicate that they are concerned about the cost. By paying attention to these non-verbal signals, you can proactively address their reservations before they become deal-breakers.

V: VALIDATE THEIR CONCERNS WITH LABELED EMPATHY

Now that you've successfully extracted your customer's reservations, it's time to validate their concerns with empathy. When archaeologists extract artifacts, they then clean the artifacts and label them so they don't lose the contextual information.

Think of validation with labeled empathy as the cleaning and labeling in the archaeological process of conservation.

To validate their concerns, use phrases like, *"I completely get the concern about <reservation>"* or *"You're not being unreasonable. It'd be a concern for me, too."* By empathizing with their reservations, you establish an emotional connection and demonstrate that you're genuinely interested in addressing their needs.

Remember, this isn't the time to jump into the problem-solving mode or become defensive. Instead, allow the customer to express their thoughts and feelings fully before moving forward.

O: OVERCOME THEIR OBJECTIONS

With the customer's reservations extracted and validated,
it's time to take the artifact to the museum. This step is all about providing the necessary information, reassurance, and support to alleviate their concerns and demonstrate the value of your product or service.

When addressing objections, come prepared with facts and data to support your claims. For example, if the customer is concerned about the cost, you can provide case studies or testimonials from other clients who have experienced a strong return on investment, or anything to reinforce the value.

Sharing success stories or examples of how your product or service has helped similar customers overcome the same concerns can be a powerful tool. It's like showing your customer a crystal ball, revealing the potential benefits for their own business.

C: CLOSE IT DOWN

Finally, the call to action. This can be anything from an assumptive close or a more direct approach to encourage the prospect to make a decision.

Once you've successfully navigated through the E.V.O., it's time to close it down, with a capital C. To close, maintain a positive and assertive tone. Reinforce the benefits of your product or service and remind the customer of the value they'll receive by choosing to move forward.

It's important to be patient and give your customer the space they need to make a decision. Avoid coming across as pushy or desperate, as this can backfire and damage the rapport you've built. Instead, exude a calm, confident demeanor that invites the customer to join you in moving forward.

In the following examples, I've listed some of the most common objections faced across many industries, and how the E.V.O.C. Method applies.

E.V.O.C. METHOD IN PRACTICE

PRICE CONCERN

Validate: *"I completely get the concern about the price. It's important that you get the best value for your money."*

Overcome: *"If you're looking for the cheapest price, in my experience, you end up buying twice. Price is offset by quality or quantity. < insert reinforced values that support your quality>. There's a reason you have an iPhone and not an entry-level Android in your hand—it's because you do have an appreciation for quality. You're in good hands."*

Close: *"If that's your only concern, let's see if we can get you qualified here (or whatever the next step looks like for you)."*

MISSING SPOUSE CONCERN

Validate: *"I can appreciate you wanting to speak with the wife before you decide. I'm married, so I get it."*

Overcome: *"What are your wife's thoughts on this? I know I've covered a lot with you, and just want to make sure she understands it just the same that led you to know it makes sense. Let's give her a shout. Fair enough?"*

Close: *"Since we couldn't reach her, let me propose this. I want to be respectful of your time. One of the core reasons I even feel comfortable asking you to make a decision now is that legally you have three business* *days to really think about it, pray about it, and discuss it with the missus before it's officially locked in. Let's get it in motion, and if she says "Hey, John, you're an idiot! Then it can be dissolved. Now, the last thing I want you to do is to cancel, so don't tell me 'yes' just for me to wrap it up, but if you're thinking you're going to do it anyway, let's knock it out while we're together. Fair enough?"*

DURABILITY CONCERN

Validate: "Your worries about the product's durability are valid. No one wants to invest in something that won't last."

Overcome: "We hired a third-party company to put that durability to the test, let me show you. And just for an extra layer of peace of mind, the warranty covers <insert any warranties or guarantees)."

Close: "From here, it's just a matter of getting your account set up. Do you have your ID on you?"

"I'M TOO OLD" (ROI) CONCERN

Validate: "I understand the concern for the return on investment. It has to make sense. "

Overcome: "When we first met, you said one of the core reasons you wanted <produce or service> is to <match the solution to the problem they wanted to be solved>. ROI doesn't factor in the emotional return on investment.*

Imagine waking up tomorrow and not having to worry about <their problem>. How would you **feel**?"

Close: "All we have to do from here is simply get you approved. What's your DOB?"

GOING INTO DEBT CONCERN

Validate: "You're not being unreasonable. It'd be a concern for me, too."

Overcome: "The challenge is, you're going to pull the trigger on a solution either today, tomorrow, or next year as the problem develops. It might as well be with the most reputable company in the industry that can lock in the terms. Here's what I'd encourage you to do. Instead of co-signing, as you had planned, let's only put it in one of your names, so the debt isn't counted against you both."

Close: "With that, is there any reason you **wouldn't** want to move forward? Perfect. Do you have your ID on you?"

NEGATIVE REVIEWS CONCERN

Validate: "Customer experience matters. It obviously matters for me."

Overcome: "There are two important topics here—one, we have over 3,000 customers. Those 13 negative reviews are

0.4% of our customers. We can pull up your favorite company, brand, or vacation destination and you'll have reviews that tell you never do business with them. When you do the volume that we do, it just comes with the territory. You can't please everyone and sometimes companies get blamed for issues that aren't even their fault or from fake competitor accounts.

Two, what I can promise you is your experience is important to me. This is my livelihood. And I can't sustain that without prioritizing you."

Close: *"I'm a big advocate for clear, consistent, and honest communication and I hope your experience so far just validates that. And if it doesn't, then it doesn't hurt my feelings. And if it does, let's get this project in motion. Fair enough?"*

COMPATIBILITY OR LEARNING CURVE CONCERN

Validate: *"I appreciate the concerns about the compatibility with the system you have now. You need seamless integration."*

Overcome: *"We have a massive team of techs that are much smarter than I am. And on the rare chance that this solution isn't viable– this is 100% risk-free to you. The most difficult thing you have to do is deal with me for a few minutes."*

Close: *"The most difficult thing you have to do is deal with me for the next few minutes. How did you want to pay?"*

ENVIRONMENTAL IMPACT CONCERN

Validate: *"I understand and share that concern as well"*

Overcome: *"Our company is really passionate about eco-friendly practices and initiatives – in fact, we spent about $xx,xxx just in the last three years in research and development to make sure those practices we've adopted are leading the way. We've got loads of info about our green initiatives that I'm more than happy to share."*

Close: *"If that's your only concern, our values are aligned. Whose name did you guys want to put this account in?"*

DATA SECURITY CONCERN

Validate: *"The data security concern is valid. I personally wouldn't want data floating out to the unknown."*

Overcome: *"The great thing about us is we have really robust security measures to protect sensitive information. We have an entire department dedicated to encryption that manages the technology, strict access controls, and routine updates. There are even third-party audits that take place to test and verify the security levels that we have."*

Close: *"We're speaking the same language here. I personally, and the company, strongly prioritize data security and privacy. I **do** have to put your info here though. What's your email?"*

CUSTOMIZATION CONCERN

Validate: *"I get the need for customization. You need a product that's robust enough to do what you need it to do."*

Overcome: *"Couple of important talking points here: one, we put the customer experience first. At the heart of that for us is simplicity and user-friendliness. Two, we have an entire team dedicated to improving that process, so feedback is taken very seriously here. Three, on the surface, it may seem less customizable, but you can integrate thousands of tools to make it as robust as you need.*

Close: *"After we get the account set up, I'll coordinate a call with our IT team to suggest and help with any integrations that can deliver what you want out of it. Where do you want me to send the agreement?"*

HIDDEN COSTS CONCERN

Validate: *"I'm just as big on transparency–I get the concern."*

Overcome: *"I can assure you that you will not find a single worm in the apple. As you can tell, I'm super comprehensive because I'd appreciate the same if I were in your shoes."*

Close: *"The only outstanding item that we haven't gotten to yet is just to make sure you can qualify. What's the last four of your social?"*

E.V.O.C. CONCLUSION

Getting to the heart of your customer's reservation is a vital aspect of the sales process. Once you've uncovered it, it's all about expressing that you have their back and bundling the information about you, your product, or your service in a value-oriented manner to overcome the reservation and seamlessly redirect the flow of the conversation to the next step. By adopting the E.V.O.C. Method at the end of your sales presentation, you'll be equipped to handle any lingering reservations or objections your customer may have to lock them down seamlessly and be on your way to disruptive levels of sales success.

Extract. Validate. Overcome. Close.

Crush it!

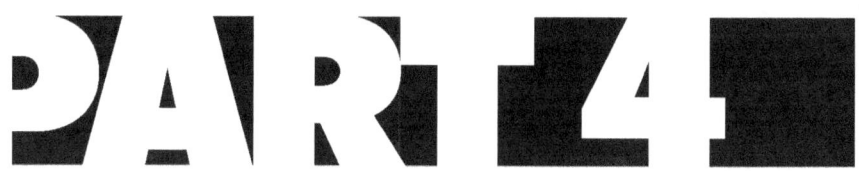

PART 4:

THE CARE CHAMP

CHAPTER 13

ENTERING THE RING: THE CARE CHAMP

On the path to disruption, the pursuit is often characterized by a relentless drive for bigger numbers and better results. Yet, beneath the surface of quotas and commissions lies a far more significant factor that separates the truly disruptive salespeople from the pack: the commitment to genuine customer care. It's this very component that keeps customers coming back to you, driving referrals, additional business, and credibility that attracts new customers.

Enter the Care Champ, the unsung hero of the sales world, and a vital part of the Triple C Path to Victory that brings the Creator, the Closer, and the Care Champ into an untouchable force of unison and total disruption. While the Creator and the Closer focus on creating opportunities and closing deals, the Care Champ takes center stage when it comes to nurturing relationships, ensuring customer satisfaction, and ultimately, sustaining exceptional levels of sales performance. In this chapter, we'll delve into the essence of the Care Champ role and explore the mindset, skills, and strategies that salespeople must adopt to achieve disruptive levels of sales success.

THE CARE CHAMP MINDSET: A COMPASSIONATE APPROACH TO SALES

At the heart of the Care Champ role lies a fundamental shift in perspective: viewing sales not as a numbers game, but as an opportunity to build meaningful connections, solve problems, and improve the lives of your customers. This mindset is perfectly captured by the African proverb, "*If you want to go fast, go alone. If you want to go far, go together.*"[1] By embracing the spirit of collaboration and focusing on the long-term success of your customers, you lay the foundation for lasting sales performance that transcends the limitations of transactional thinking.

To embody the Care Champ mindset, salespeople must cultivate the following qualities:

EMPATHY

The ability to genuinely understand and appreciate the needs, concerns, and emotions of your customers, and to use this insight to inform your sales approach.

SERVICE-ORIENTED ATTITUDE

A commitment to going above and beyond in meeting the needs of your customers, regardless of whether a sale is directly involved.

AUTHENTICITY

Bleeding over from the other roles, the willingness to be genuine, honest, and transparent in your interactions, building trust, and fostering strong relationships with your customers.

ADAPTABILITY

The capacity to stay nimble and responsive in the face of changing customer needs, market conditions, and industry trends, ensures that your sales approach remains relevant and effective.

THE CARE CHAMP TOOLKIT: SKILLS AND STRATEGIES FOR CUSTOMER-CENTRIC SUCCESS

With the Care Champ mindset firmly in place, salespeople can begin to develop the skills and strategies necessary to excel in this crucial role. The following are some key areas of focus for those looking to become true Care Champs:

ACTIVE LISTENING

The ability to fully engage with your customers, paying close attention to their words, emotions, and body language, and using this information to tailor your sales approach to their unique needs and preferences. As the Chinese proverb goes, "To listen well is as powerful a means of communication and influence as to talk well."

EFFECTIVE COMMUNICATION

The capacity to convey your message clearly, persuasively, and with genuine care, ensuring that your customers feel valued, understood, and confident in their decision-making process.

RELATIONSHIP BUILDING

The skill of forging deep, meaningful connections with your customers, fostering a sense of loyalty and trust that leads to long-term sales success.

PROBLEM-SOLVING

The ability to identify and address the challenges and pain points faced by your customers, offering innovative solutions that not only meet their needs but also enhance their overall experience with your business.

FOLLOW-UP AND AFTER-SALES SUPPORT

The commitment to maintaining regular contact with your customers, providing ongoing support, and addressing any concerns or issues that may arise, ensuring their continued satisfaction and loyalty.

LEVERAGING CUSTOMER CARE FOR BUSINESS GROWTH

The art of harnessing your reputation for exceptional customer care to attract new clients, generate referrals and fuel the expansion of your business.

THE ROAD TO BECOMING A CARE CHAMP: A JOURNEY OF CONTINUOUS GROWTH

Embarking on the path to becoming a Care Champ is not a one-time event, but rather a journey of continuous growth and self-improvement. Salespeople who embrace this role must be prepared to evolve with the changing needs of their customers, refine their skills, and adapt their strategies in pursuit of ever-greater levels of sales success.

INVEST IN ONGOING LEARNING AND DEVELOPMENT

Seek opportunities to expand your knowledge, sharpen your skills, and stay informed about the latest trends and best practices in customer care. This may include attending workshops, reading industry publications, or participating in online forums and communities.

SEEK FEEDBACK AND EMBRACE CONSTRUCTIVE CRITICISM

Solicit input from your customers, peers, and mentors, and be open to the insights and suggestions they provide. Use this feedback to refine your approach, address any weaknesses, and build upon your strengths as a Care Champ.

SET CLEAR GOALS AND TRACK YOUR PROGRESS

Establish measurable objectives for your customer care efforts, such as increasing customer satisfaction scores or reducing churn rates, and regularly monitor your progress towards these goals. This will help you identify areas for improvement and maintain your focus on continuous growth.

CELEBRATE YOUR SUCCESSES AND LEARN FROM YOUR MISTAKES

Recognize and reward yourself for the milestones you achieve in your journey to becoming a Care Champ, and use any setbacks or challenges as opportunities to learn and grow. Crash seven times, rise eight – because gravity is just a tree in the way of the most epic soar.

In conclusion, the Care Champ role represents a transformative approach to sales that prioritizes genuine customer care, going above and beyond to meet their needs and exceed their expectations. By incorporating the Care Champ role into your collection of disruptive wearing hats, developing the necessary skills and strategies, and committing to a journey of continuous growth, you can unlock the full potential of the Triple C Path to Victory, achieving disruptive levels of sales success and leaving a lasting legacy of care in their wake.

Remember that the road to becoming a Care Champ is paved with the stories of the lives you've touched, the problems you've solved, and the relationships you've built. Embrace this journey with open arms, and you'll find that the rewards of a customer-centric approach to sales extend far beyond the bottom line, enriching both your professional and personal life.

CHAPTER 14

THE CARE CHAMP'S JAB AND UPPERCUT

The Care Champ's role is key to building long-lasting relationships, driving customer loyalty, and achieving disruptive sales success. But what's the secret of your disruptive sales leader that transcends above the average traditional salesperson? Imagine a world where the concept of customer service is just a myth, an elusive creature, like a mother of three tiny tornados, navigating the chaos with the grace of a ballerina and *zero caffeine*. In this world, the responsibility of providing exceptional customer experiences falls squarely on your shoulders, with no safety net to catch you. This is precisely the mindset that the Care Champ, the beacon of disruptive sales success, must embrace. The jab is swift, yet powerful: **pretend that customer service doesn't exist**.

By adopting this mindset, you effectively remove any potential crutch that might tempt you to fall short in delivering unparalleled customer experiences. The idea is that when there's a department designated to handle customer complaints and issues, it's all too easy to become complacent, allowing mediocrity to seep into your sales process. And as a wise Japanese proverb goes, "Vision without action is a daydream; action without vision is a nightmare."[1] In other words, merely knowing the importance of excellent customer care is not enough. You must put it into practice.

When mediocrity creeps in, it gradually erodes your ability to maintain high levels of sales performance, which is a necessity for any successful sales professional. So, how do you embody the Care Champ mindset and adhere to this rule of pretending customer service doesn't exist?

OWN THE CUSTOMER EXPERIENCE

As a Care Champ, you must take full responsibility for every interaction you have with your customers, from the initial contact to the follow-up after the sale. This holistic approach ensures that you are always striving to provide the best possible experience, without relying on others to pick up the slack.

EMBRACE PROACTIVITY

Don't wait for customers to reach out with their issues or concerns. Instead, be proactive in identifying potential problems and addressing them before they escalate. By staying one step ahead of your customers' needs, you can demonstrate your commitment to their satisfaction and build lasting relationships.

DEVELOP YOUR PROBLEM-SOLVING SKILLS

When confronted with customer concerns, channel your inner Sherlock Holmes and get to the root of the issue. By honing your problem-solving abilities, you can address customer needs more effectively and efficiently, without passing the accountability baton to another department.

CONTINUOUSLY IMPROVE YOUR COMMUNICATION

Excellent communication is the foundation of any great customer experience. Focus on sharpening your listening and empathy skills, so you can better understand your customers and respond to their needs in a way that fosters trust and loyalty.

EMBODY THE VALUES OF YOUR BRAND

As a Care Champ, you are the face of your company to your customers. Ensure that your actions, words, and demeanor align with your organization's values and mission. By embodying these principles, you can create an authentic and consistent customer experience that reflects your brand's unique identity.

ADOPT A SERVICE-ORIENTED ATTITUDE

Strive to cultivate a mindset that prioritizes service above all else. As the Hasworth proverb goes, "if you believe being small means you can't make an impact, you've obviously never experienced the sheer force of a solitary, determined popcorn hull to stay between teeth." Every interaction, no matter how seemingly insignificant, can have a profound impact on your customer's perception of your business.

APPROACH EVERY INTERACTION WITH THE GOAL OF EXCEEDING THEIR EXPECTATIONS.

By pretending that customer service doesn't exist, you effectively shift the responsibility of providing exceptional care onto yourself. This mindset forces you to go above and beyond in every customer interaction, ensuring that you not only meet but exceed their expectations. In turn, this commitment to excellence will help you stand out from the competition, driving referrals, repeat business, and long-term growth.

In conclusion, embracing the Care Champ's first rule of pretending customer service doesn't exist is a powerful strategy for achieving disruptive sales success. By owning the customer experience, being proactive, honing your problem-solving and communication skills, and adopting a service-oriented attitude, you can cultivate the mindset and habits that will propel you to the upper echelons of sales performance. After all, the road to success is perpetually under construction, complete with traffic cones, detours, and the occasional jackhammer. So, roll up your sleeves, grab your hard hat, and start building your path to disruptive sales success with the Care Champ mindset.

DON'T TURN YOUR CUSTOMER INTO YOUR OPPONENT

If the Care Champ's first rule is the roots of an oak, then this second rule is the nourishing soil that promotes its growth. Derived from Donald Miller's golden rule of never badmouthing a customer[2], this rule emphasizes the importance of maintaining a positive attitude and focusing on empathy, even in the face of difficult customer interactions. Simply put, don't turn your customer into your opponent, no matter how badly they want to fight.

To truly embody the Care Champ role, it's essential to understand the reasoning behind this rule, how it can be applied in various situations, and the impact it can have on your sales performance.

WHY TURNING CUSTOMERS INTO OPPONENTS IS COUNTERPRODUCTIVE

It's not uncommon for salespeople to encounter challenging customers who are hard to please or may have unreasonable demands. In these moments, it might be tempting to vent your frustrations or blame the customer for their behavior. However, it's about as productive as a porcupine in a balloon factory. Doing so is not only unprofessional, but it can also create a toxic environment that hinders your ability to achieve exceptional sales results.

Turning customers into opponents fosters a negative mindset, which can be contagious among your team members, leading to a decrease in morale and motivation. Furthermore, badmouthing a customer reflects poorly on your character and can damage your reputation as a trusted and top-performing sales professional. It's essential to remember that every customer interaction is an opportunity to learn, grow, and hone your skills as a Care Champ.

The tongue's got skills even a thousand hands can't compete with. I'll wait... Now that you've gotten that *"that's what she said"* out of your system, in all seriousness, your words carry immense power, and using them carelessly can lead to lasting damage that cannot be undone.

TIPS FOR TRAINING THE MIND & TAMING THE TONGUE

As a Care Champ, it's vital to cultivate a habit of using positive language and reframing challenging situations into opportunities for growth. While the goal is to shift our language, it starts with our thought process. So, here are a few examples of thought transformation:

BEING UNREASONABLE

When you think: "*This customer is so difficult and unreasonable. I don't know why they're making such a big deal out of this issue.*"

Shift your thinking to: "*This customer is clearly passionate about resolving their issue. What's their perspective here?*"

Looking at it from their perspective can help you look through the frustration and gain insight into what's causing it. This allows you to shift to a solutions-oriented frame of mind.

LEAVING TO JOIN A COMPETITOR

When you think: "*I can't believe this customer is leaving us for a competitor. After all that I've done for them! They clearly don't appreciate all the effort we've put into helping them.*"

Shift your thinking to: *"That's disappointing. What would drive this customer to want to leave after the effort we put into them?"*

Explore any feedback that was left that led a customer to jump ship, extracting valuable data that can help you evolve and prevent similar situations from happening with additional customers.

WAITING TIME/ISN'T GOING TO BUY

When you think: *"This is the worst customer - they've been in twice just to look around and leave."*

Shift your thinking to: *"I have to convert this customer. Let me see what information they're just not getting that's preventing them from making a decision."*

EMBRACING THE CARE CHAMP MINDSET

By adhering to the Care Champ's rule of never turning your customer into an opponent, you demonstrate a commitment to maintaining a positive outlook, fostering empathy, and prioritizing the customer's needs. This mindset not only benefits your relationships with customers but also contributes to a healthier, more supportive work environment.

To embody the Care Champ role, it's essential to practice self-awareness and continuously strive to improve your communication skills. Consider seeking feedback from colleagues or participating in sales training programs to help you fine-tune your approach to challenging customer interactions.

In the end, the ability to refrain from badmouthing customers and maintain a positive attitude is a testament to your professionalism and dedication to delivering exceptional customer care. By embracing this, you'll be better equipped to navigate difficult situations, maintain strong relationships with your customers, and ultimately drive your sales performance to new heights.

Here are a few more tips to help you avoid turning customers into opponents and stay true to the Care Champ role:

PRACTICE ACTIVE LISTENING

When dealing with customers, it's important to genuinely listen to their concerns, needs, and feedback. Listening is just as important as talking. The same way you wouldn't eat a perfectly good bowl of "Oops, All Berries" without the right balance of your favorite milk is the same way you can't enjoy the full flavor of a conversation without both ingredients in the mix. By actively listening, you'll be better equipped to understand their perspective and respond empathetically.

AVOID MAKING ASSUMPTIONS

It's easy to jump to conclusions and assume a customer is being difficult or unreasonable. Instead, try to approach each interaction with an open mind and focus on understanding the root cause of their concerns.

KEEP YOUR EMOTIONS IN CHECK

It's natural to feel frustrated or upset when faced with a challenging customer. However, it's crucial to remain calm and composed in these situations. Taking a few deep breaths or momentarily stepping away from the situation can help you regain your composure.

FOCUS ON SOLUTIONS

Instead of dwelling on the negative aspects of customer interactions, shift your focus towards finding a solution that addresses their needs and concerns. This proactive approach demonstrates your commitment to helping the customer and reinforces the Care Champ mindset.

LEARN FROM EACH EXPERIENCE

Every customer interaction, whether positive or negative, presents an opportunity to learn and grow as a sales professional. Reflect on your interactions with customers and identify areas where you can improve your communication, empathy, and problem-solving skills.

In conclusion, this rule is the cornerstone of a customer-centric sales approach that drives disruptive results. By adhering to this rule and continually working to improve your communication and empathy skills, you'll be well on your way to becoming a true Care Champ, knocking out the most challenging goals. Remember, the customer may not always be right, but treating them with respect and understanding will go a long way in building trust, and loyalty, and fostering long-term business relationships.

Conclusion

As you have likely gathered by now, achieving disruptive success in the world of sales requires a more profound, holistic perspective, embracing not only the transactional aspect but also cultivating a mindset and skillset that foster excellence. I passionately admit that I am still on this journey of growth. As we ride it together, it's crucial to understand that, at the highest levels of performance, numbers are not the ultimate destination. Percentages on a spreadsheet only serve as a yardstick for others to judge and rank us, not for us to rank us. There is no percentage to achieve or destination to arrive to. There is only an everlasting journey with no destination in sight– just taking in the landscape as we ascend to the top, with a plethora of newfound tweet-sized quotes, and a copy of this book in the passenger seat.

Learn. Elevate. Disrupt.

NOTES

Introduction

[1]Mamet, David. Glengarry Glen Ross. 1984.

Chapter 1 | Mindset Matters

[1]Haynes, C. (2018, March 15). Stephen Curry: Mental part of the game 'just as important as the physical'. ESPN. Retrieved from https://www.espn.com/nba/story/_/id/22766882/stephen-curry-golden-state-warriors-says-mental-part-game-just-important-physical

Chapter 2 | Toss The Split Wires

[1]Hatfield, Elaine, John T. Cacioppo, and Richard L. Rapson. Emotional Contagion. Cambridge University Press, 1994.

[2]Díaz del Castillo, Bernal. The Conquest of New Spain. Translated by J. M. Cohen, Penguin Books, 1963.

Chapter 3 | Subconscious Transformation

[1]Fleet, Thurman. Rays of the Dawn: Natural Laws of the Body, Mind and Soul. Concept-Therapy International, 1970.

[2]Proctor, Bob, and Sandra Gallagher. Thoughts Become Things. LifeSuccess Publishing, 2015.

[3]Cowan, Nelson. "The Magical Number 4 in Short-Term Memory: A Reconsideration of Mental Storage Capacity." Behavioral and Brain Sciences, vol. 24, no. 1, 2001, pp. 87-114.

[4]Savage, Kyra Bobinet, and Robin Berzin. "The Neuroscience of Behavior Change." Health Transformer, Medium, 29 June 2018, https://healthtransformer.co/the-neuroscience-of-behavior-change-bcb567fa83c1.

[5]Catherine Ford. "Hedge fund billionaire Ray Dalio: Meditation is 'the single most important reason for my success.", Yahoo News, March 16, 2018, https://www.yahoo.com/news/hedge-fund-billionaire-ray-dalio-192800564.html

Chapter 4 | The Creator's Rule

[1]Patton, George S. "A good plan violently executed now is better than a perfect plan executed next week." Quoted in Rick Atkinson, An Army at Dawn: The War in North Africa, 1942-1943. Henry Holt and Company, 2002.

[2]Seetharaman, Deepa. "Reddit Claims 52 Million Daily Users, Revealing a Key Figure for Social Media Platforms." The Wall Street Journal, Dow Jones & Company, 1 Dec. 2020, https://www.wsj.com/articles/reddit-claims-52-million-daily-users-revealing-a-key-figure-for-social-media-platforms-11606822200.

[3]Reddit. "Reddit: The Front Page of the Internet." https://www.reddit.com/. Accessed 22 Mar. 2023.

[4]Koebler, Jason. "How Reddit Got Huge: Tons of Fake Accounts." Vice, Vice Media, 4 Feb. 2014, https://www.vice.com/en/article/z4444w/how-reddit-got-huge-tons-of-fake-accounts--2.

Chapter 5 | The Four Elements of Communication

[1]Carnegie, Dale. How to Win Friends and Influence People. Simon and Schuster, 1936.

[2]Kitts, Kea Norrell-Aitch. "Eye Contact: Don't Make These Mistakes." Michigan State University Extension, 29 Mar. 2018, https://www.canr.msu.edu/news/eye_contact_dont_make_these_mistakes#:~:text=To%20mai

ntain%20appropriate%20eye%20contact,it%20for%204%

2D5%20seconds.

[3]Pfeffer, Ronald E. "There's Magic in Your Smile."
Psychology Today, Sussex Publishers, 25 June 2012,
https://www.psychologytoday.com/us/blog/cutting-edge-
leadership/201206/there-s-magic-in-your-smile.

Chapter 6 | Starting from Zero - The 100-Shot Shakeup

[1]nTelos Wireless. "GREAT Process." 2010.

Chapter 7 | Opportunity Optimization

[1]Spotify. "Spotify Premium: Ad-Free Experience." https://
www.spotify.com/premium/. Accessed 22 Mar. 2023.

[2]Apple Inc. "Apple Store: 'You May Also Like'" https://
www.apple.com/shop/. Accessed 22 Mar. 2023.

[3]McDonald's. "McDonald's Upsell Strategy: 'Would You
Like to Make That a Combo?'" https://
www.mcdonalds.com/. Accessed 22 Mar. 2023.

[4]Amazon. "Amazon Checkout: Frequently Bought Together and Customers Who Bought This Item Also Bought." https://www.amazon.com/. Accessed 22 Mar. 2023.

[5]Cohn, Chuck. "A Beginner's Guide to Upselling and Cross-Selling." Forbes, 15 May 2015, https://www.forbes.com/sites/chuckcohn/2015/05/15/a-beginners-guide-to-upselling-and-cross-selling/?sh=6396a4b12912.

[6]CVS Pharmacy. "ExtraCare Loyalty Program." https://www.cvs.com/extracare/. Accessed 22 Mar. 2023.

[7]Starbucks Corporation. "Starbucks Rewards Program." https://www.starbucks.com/rewards/. Accessed 22 Mar. 2023.

[8]Golden Goose. "App-Exclusive Shoe Designs." https://www.goldengoosedeluxebrand.com/. Accessed 22 Mar. 2023.

[9]LinkedIn Corporation. "LinkedIn Premium Program Offer." https://www.linkedin.com/premium/. Accessed 22 Mar. 2023.

[10]LinkedIn Corporation. "About LinkedIn: User and Membership Metrics." https://about.linkedin.com/. Accessed 22 Mar. 2023.

Chapter 8 | The Closer's Rulebook: 10 Closer Commandments

[1]Cialdini, Robert B. Influence: The Psychology of Persuasion. HarperCollins, 1984.

Chapter 9 | Elevation in Observation

[1]Isaacson, Walter. Steve Jobs. Simon & Schuster, 2011.

[2]Stone, Brad. The Everything Store: Jeff Bezos and the Age of Amazon. Little, Brown and Company, 2013. Levy, Steven. In the [2]Plex: How Google Thinks, Works, and Shapes Our Lives. Simon & Schuster, 2011.

[3]Keating, Gina. Netflixed: The Epic Battle for America's Eyeballs. Portfolio/Penguin, 2012.

[4]Vance, Ashlee. Elon Musk: Tesla, SpaceX, and the Quest for a Fantastic Future. Ecco, 2015. Ford, Henry, and Samuel Crowther. My Life and Work. Doubleday, Page & Company, 1922.

[5]Ghemawat, Pankaj, and José Luis Nueno. "ZARA: Fast Fashion." Harvard Business School Case 703-497, April 2003 (Revised August 2006). Liker, Jeffrey K. The Toyota Way: 14 Management Principles from the World's Greatest Manufacturer. McGraw-Hill, 2004.

Chapter 10 | The Closer's Ascension

[1]Plato. "Apology." The Dialogues of Plato, translated by Benjamin Jowett, Oxford University Press, 1892.

[2]Lao Tzu. Tao Te Ching, translated by Stephen Mitchell, Harper Perennial, 1988.

Chapter 11 | F.I.N.D. Your Customer

[1]Kahneman, Daniel, and Amos Tversky. "Judgment under Uncertainty: Heuristics and Biases." Science, vol. 185, no. 4157, 1974, pp. 1124-1131.
The best sales book ever.

Chapter 12 | Mastering The Close: The E.V.O.C. Method

Chapter 13 | Entering The Ring: The Care Champ

[1]African Proverb. "If you want to go fast, go alone. If you want to go far, go together."

Chapter 14 | The Care Champ's Jab and Uppercut

[1]Japanese Proverb. "Vision without action is a daydream; action without vision is a nightmare."

[2]Miller, Donald. "Donald Miller's Golden Rule of Customer Service: Never Badmouthing a Customer." YouTube, uploaded by Business Made Simple, 5 July. 2019, https://www.youtube.com/watch?v=hBjKw2gasik.

ABOUT THE AUTHOR

Kash Hasworth is a prominent and experienced leader in sales, marketing, culture development, and scalability, with a fierce passion for relentless execution and disruptive results. After scaling a wireless franchise to staggering 28 locations, he dove headfirst into the renewable energy arena. Earning his wings from ground level in a new industry, Kash rapidly climbed to the #1 spot in personal sales for one of the largest solar companies in the nation in his first year, displaying great strengths of adaptability and universal sales application.

Now serving as Solar Ignite Group founder and CEO, he's on a mission to help elevate others, as he takes his years of experience and pours it into an easily digestible and actionable book to give readers a guided path to catapult to the forefront of their industry in the most efficient and effective way possible.

@KASHHASWORTH | KASHHASWORTH.COM